"In an increasingly disconnected world, *The Way Back to One Another* stands out as one of the most important and powerful books I've read. Jeff, Phil, and Jill have masterfully woven together Scripture, personal stories, the wisdom of the global church, and practical steps to foster the connection God created us to enjoy. This book doesn't just diagnose the ache of loneliness—it offers a clear, hope-filled path toward building interdependent, Christ-centered communities that truly transform lives. If you're longing for relationships that go beyond the surface, this book will meet you with wisdom, warmth, and a way forward into the joy of authentic community."
Peter Greer, president and CEO of HOPE International

"God's word is clear. He calls and empowers his people to a one-another life of love and fellowship, but we are too often captured by the same polarizations that permeate our world. I am thankful that Jeff Galley and Phil Smith have given us *The Way Back to One Another*. This practical resource, grounded in Scripture, shows us the way to beautiful community for the glory of God."
Irwyn L. Ince Jr., author of *The Beautiful Community* and *Hope Ain't a Hustle*

"This book is a timely and powerful reminder that we are not only created for connection but need it in order to flourish. The stories beautifully illustrate how meeting practical needs can also awaken and satisfy our deeper longing to belong, to be seen, and to walk together through life. Throughout the book, the authors invite readers to reflect, engage in meaningful conversations, and take practical steps toward cultivating a community where the one-anothers are lived out. Page by page, I was reawakened to my own need for others and equipped with tangible ways to pursue those around me."
Jackie E. Perry, professor of counselor education at Columbia International University and creator of The Attuned Listener Course

"I couldn't put this book down. In a world where we scroll past one another more than we sit beside each other, *The Way Back to One Another* feels like both a diagnosis and a cure. Through stories that span continents and faith communities, Jeff Galley and Phil Smith remind us of what we've forgotten: that the gospel is not just personal; it's profoundly communal. This is a deeply hopeful, deeply needed work—one that reclaims the radical simplicity of Jesus' command to 'love one another.' It's a call to remember who we are and to rebuild what we've lost: a church marked not by production, but by presence; not by programs, but by people. I'll be recommending this book to every leader I know who cares about spiritual formation, belonging, and the future of the church."
Mandy Arioto, president and CEO of MomCo Global

"Social media offers ample opportunities for connectivity, and yet the sense of loneliness among people has increased. *The Way Back to One Another* offers insights into this puzzling trend and provides practical tips and biblical knowledge to address the epidemic of loneliness. God has created us with an intrinsic need for belonging, and the authors gently guide us back to the richness of a *koinōnia* community."

Ling Dinse, department chair of social work at Messiah University

"After living in East Africa for more than a decade, I've seen what it looks like when community is not just an ideal but a way of life. In a cultural moment when isolation, anxiety, and disconnection are rising at an alarming rate, Jeff Galley and Phil Smith offer us a timely and necessary reminder: God created us for relationship. This book is a clarion call for a return to the shared life we were made for—not merely a strategy, but a way of being. We would do well to listen."

Coy Buckley, president and CEO of the Chalmers Center for Economic Development

THE WAY BACK
TO ONE ANOTHER

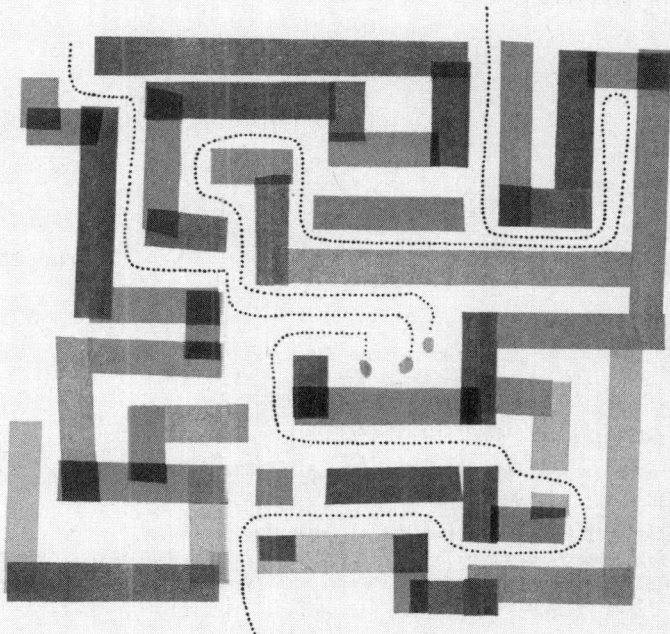

How to Live as People
Created for Community

JEFF GALLEY and **PHILLIP N. SMITH**

WITH JILL HEISEY

FOREWORD BY CRAIG GROESCHEL

ivp

An imprint of InterVarsity Press
Downers Grove, Illinois

InterVarsity Press
P.O. Box 1400 | Downers Grove, IL 60515-1426
ivpress.com | email@ivpress.com

Cover design: Faceout Studio, Molly von Borstel
Interior design: Jeanna Wiggins

ISBN 978-1-5140-1440-0 (print) | ISBN 978-1-5140-1441-7 (digital)

Printed in the United States of America ∞

Library of Congress Cataloging-in-Publication Data
A catalog record for this book is available from the Library of Congress.

33 32 31 30 29 28 27 26 | 13 12 11 10 9 8 7 6 5 4 3 2 1

For the countless savings group members across the globe,

whose courage, generosity, and commitment to each other have

shown us what community the way God intended looks like.

You've inspired us not just to write about your experiences

but to seek that same togetherness in our own lives.

With profound gratitude,

PHIL AND JEFF

CONTENTS

FOREWORD

CRAIG GROESCHEL

WHEN MY DAD PASSED AWAY IN 2023, my wife Amy and I were overwhelmed by the expressions of love that poured in from those in our community and around the world. There were thousands of comments on social media, over a hundred emails in my inbox, and dozens of texts. Beautiful bouquets arrived as tangible expressions of love, and we knew without a doubt that we were held in the thoughts and prayers of many. But something was missing.

Almost every interaction was devoid of personal voice and personal presence. In the first week, only two friends called to personally express their sorrow for our loss. Just one, my childhood friend Scott, drove to our house, knocked on my door, and asked, "How are you?"—and honestly, it felt somewhat odd. Almost no one knocks on a door unannounced nowadays. "How are *you*?" I responded, not fully grasping the intent of his visit. "Is something wrong?"

Something is wrong.

God never intended showing up for one another to be an anomaly, but in today's relational economy it is. The loss of connection, personal touch, and genuine intimacy is a loss we're collectively grieving. A recent Harvard University study shows that one in three people believe they have needs but no one to meet them, hurts but no one to listen, and love to give but no one to receive it. Too many of us feel relationally impoverished, and God says that's not a good way to live (Genesis 2:18).

The early church got this. Acts 2:46 says the first-century believers met together every day. Together, they confronted persecution, economic hardship, and sickness. Together, they waged a spiritual battle against an enemy who came to steal, kill, and destroy. They united around the Word of God, lifting one another up, strengthening each other, and being the body of Christ in a world that needed Jesus. First-century Christians desperately needed each other, and they knew it. Modern-day believers need each other but have forgotten it.

Mental health experts say that most people across the United States seek autonomy and independence. In doing so, we are intentionally pursuing a life that destroys our mental health and robs us of real joy and lasting fulfillment. We're intentionally pursuing a life outside God's design.

In the miracle and mystery of the Trinity, God himself is a perfect community, and it's a gift he desires to share with us. God didn't create us because he was lonely; he created us because he is love, and one of the primary ways we experience God's love is through loving one another. God bears your burdens, meets your needs, and heals you—often through other people.

But true, lasting, and ongoing intimacy with other people rarely happens accidentally. True intimacy takes intentionality. Thankfully, Jeff and Phil's book *The Way Back to One Another* offers us a scripturally grounded, intentional plan for spiritual strength in community. Like loving guides, they invite us to rediscover God's rich design for community. They invite the church to assume our God-given role in combating the loneliness epidemic and call us to both a personal and communal vision of what could be when we love one another. In a culture that distances others, I know this book will help us draw together.

AUTHORS' NOTE

PROCEEDS FROM THE SALE OF THIS BOOK will benefit the following organizations that are actively pursuing the way back to one another. Their work in alleviating both physical and relational poverty inspires us, and we've been privileged to see how God is working through them to create the type of vibrant, Christ-centered communities we highlight within this book.

HOPE INTERNATIONAL
hopeinternational.org

HOPE International invests in the dreams of families in the world's underserved communities as they proclaim and live the gospel.

HOPE serves as a network of microfinance institutions and savings group programs in Africa, Asia, Eastern Europe, and Latin America. As men and women around the world engage with HOPE, they hear the good news of Jesus and access biblically based training, a safe place to save, and business loans that help them overcome material and spiritual poverty.

GLOBAL LIFT COLLECTIVE
globallift.org

Global Lift Collective is a group of churches and NGO partners working together to abolish extreme poverty and unleash the God-given potential of all people.

The Collective dreams for every church to lead the way in holistically transforming their community, beginning with a current focus in Malawi and Central America.

Global Lift Collective resourcing partners include many churches in the United States, Canada, and the United Kingdom facilitated by Life.Church in Oklahoma City, Oklahoma; Willow Creek Community Church in Chicago; and Northridge Church in Rochester, New York. Global Lift Collective NGO program partners include Tearfund, HOPE International, World Relief, Enlace, and Living Water International.

THE CHALMERS CENTER FOR ECONOMIC DEVELOPMENT

chalmers.org

The Chalmers Center for Economic Development helps God's people rethink poverty and respond with practical, biblical principles so that all are restored to flourishing. Through bestselling books like *When Helping Hurts*, transformative training programs, and partnerships with churches and ministries around the world, Chalmers has equipped thousands of leaders to implement effective poverty alleviation strategies and reached more than three million people globally with a biblical approach to poverty alleviation.

WORLD RELIEF

wr.org

World Relief is a global Christian humanitarian organization whose mission is to boldly engage the world's greatest crises in partnership with the church. The organization was founded in the aftermath of World War II to respond to the urgent humanitarian needs of war-torn Europe. Since then, for over eighty years, across one hundred countries, World Relief has partnered with local churches and communities to build a world where families thrive and communities flourish. Today, organizational programming focuses on humanitarian and disaster response as well as community strengthening and resilience.

LONGING FOR SOMETHING MORE

I (PHIL) HAVE MOVED FIFTEEN TIMES in my four decades of marriage to my wife, Becca. We have lived in six states, four countries, and three continents. We're richer for the experience, but it hasn't been easy. We've left the familiar and discovered the new fifteen times. We've cried through gut-wrenching goodbyes and summoned the courage for another round of hellos: trying to build relationships and find community in each new setting.

Sometimes we've met quick success. In Connecticut, the first church we visited embraced us from the moment we arrived. When the service concluded, we were invited to a lunch gathering at one attendee's home. About twenty people came together to eat and enjoy one another's company while the kids ran wild. We felt right at home—and the feeling lasted as we built ever-deepening relationships in this church community.

On our relocation to another state, Becca expressed her desire for friendship to a coworker who was a lifelong resident. "This is a special place," the woman responded knowingly. "It will take you ten years to make close friends here, but once you have them, they're yours for life." We lasted just under a year in this town, so we never had the opportunity to test the theory that a decade of investment would yield lifelong returns.

In my career journey, I'd already transitioned from corporate executive to executive pastor, but in 2006, I made another significant pivot to the nonprofit sector. Becca and I moved to Rwanda, where she turned our home's extra bedrooms into an extraordinary guesthouse that welcomed a steady stream of visitors, and I served as country director with World Relief, a Christian humanitarian organization that brings sustainable solutions to problems like global poverty.

I've often wondered if searching for home in so many new places has heightened my awareness of the universal longing for meaningful relationships and connection. I observed it in the United States, England, Canada, and Rwanda. I saw it in corner offices, in wooden pews, in people walking through divorce, depression, grief, addictions, job loss, and parenting challenges. In people living without a sense of belonging and a community of support. In myself. I felt it despite being raised in a loving family and close-knit congregation. I regularly longed for a community that would share my joy and, in darker seasons of my life, help me bear burdens too heavy to shoulder alone.

During the years Becca and I spent in Rwanda, the community we observed went further and deeper in their care and support than any we had previously seen or experienced. It wasn't uncommon for a group of friends to make an unannounced visit to someone's home—no special occasion, no illness, just to visit and enjoy being together. The first time friends arrived on our doorstep unannounced, it felt intrusive and impolite. Couldn't they call first? Didn't they know we had things to do? In our early days in Rwanda, a colleague regularly reminded me of the African proverb, "Westerners have watches; Africans have time."

As difficult as it was to shed our cultural bent toward our schedules and plans, over time we grew to love and value these surprise visits, pausing whatever we were doing to welcome and enjoy friends. In fact, the visits took me back to childhood memories of my parents welcoming unexpected guests who'd dropped by to say hello. It seemed a lot had changed in just one generation!

The depth of community we experienced in Rwanda sparked my continuing curiosity, *What is it about some folks that makes Jesus' words come to life?*: "Your love for one another will prove to the world that you are my disciples" (John 13:35 NLT).

This question continued to solidify when I later accepted a role as HOPE International's director of savings groups. Back in the United States, I worked to empower the local church in Rwanda and many other countries throughout Africa, Asia, Eastern Europe, and Latin America to form groups that would save small sums of money together to create an emergency fund or investment fund to finance small enterprises or significant expenses like children's school fees.

Savings groups are foreign to our thinking in the Western world because we have access to basic financial services. But organizations like HOPE International, World Relief, Tearfund, and the Chalmers Center use savings groups as a sustainable tool for equipping and empowering those in the developing world who have no access to formal financial services and are living in poverty, including many who meet the criteria for extreme poverty, living on less than three dollars per day.[1] In the models used by all the aforementioned organizations, savings groups are a Christ-centered ministry of the local church.

With guidance, training, and mentoring from local church volunteers, savings groups of roughly fifteen to twenty-five members form and govern themselves. They determine their membership, elect officers, create their own rules, decide when they meet and how much they save, and more. Most meet weekly. No capital is injected from the outside. Instead, members steward and multiply what they already have, no matter how limited.

Participants join these groups to experience financial transformation, but over time most become even more eager to share about the *relational* transformation they've experienced. Again and again, across vastly differing cultures, I heard things like, "Before we began, we were isolated . . . alone . . . lonely. We had nothing; we were ignored and forgotten. Now we are like a family. We care for each other. Nobody could ever separate us."

Isolation is a global problem, but each of these globally dispersed groups seemed to have overcome it. While members spoke of their loneliness and isolation before joining the group, now there was a sense of togetherness. How did that happen? How did they arrive at such deep love for each other? Was it a short-lived social phenomenon or lasting? Was it unique to those escaping poverty together or could it be replicated in other contexts? Fundamentally, *could I recreate a rich, isolation-defying community like this in my own life?*

A Parallel Journey (Jeff's Story)

Over fifteen years ago, a friend introduced me (Jeff) to the work of development experts Brian Fikkert and Steve Corbett and their book *When Helping Hurts*. Because I oversee small groups and select and evaluate ministry partners for Life.Church, I deeply resonated with the authors' call to ensure that our "help" is truly helping. Several ideas in the book were formative, but most impactful of all was Fikkert and Corbett's assertion that the simple act of building a relationship can be life-changing. A relationship is a goal in itself, not a means to an end. This revelation brought together in my mind what had felt like two distinct roles I held at Life.Church: facilitating connections and facilitating human development. The two were intrinsically linked.

Influenced in no small way by Fikkert and Corbett's thinking, writing, and direct endorsement, Life.Church sought out a partnership with HOPE International's savings group ministry. I knew from the research that savings groups have a track record of catalyzing economic transformation. Still, there was an element of a savings group that I did not understand until I had the privilege of visiting one for the first time over a decade ago. From that first visit, I was blown away by the power of community within these groups.

Economic transformation notwithstanding, the power of these groups is, as Corbett and Fikkert asserted, in the relationships. They transform the families involved and their surrounding community because members know, love, and trust each other—shortcomings, imperfections, and all. This realization sparked a longing within me for the same kind of transformative community in my own life. Phil and I spoke at length about the groups, but in the context of our professional relationship, our longing to distill and apply the same principles to our own lives was never part of the discussion.

Several years later, after meeting and working closely with Phil and deepening the partnership between our organizations, I was invited to share devotions with a group of HOPE supporters. As I pondered and prayed over what to share, I knew that I wanted to tell the story of relationships.

I used my devotions to encourage HOPE's supporters to follow the lead of savings group members in creating the same kind of safety and community within our spheres of influence: our homes, workplaces, and churches.

Phil rushed up to me as soon as I'd finished sharing. "We need to talk!" he said. I immediately began retracing my words, wondering how I'd misspoken to provoke such a passionate reaction. Instead, Phil told me I was speaking his heart—and more or less plagiarizing a book that he'd already begun writing. He invited me to consider partnering with him to communicate our shared passion to see men and women rediscover the God-given gift of community.

Journey of Discovery

We've spent the last few years contemplating the gift of community and the pain of its absence. Both of us have had wonderful experiences with community here in the United States. But, if we're honest, those experiences pale in comparison to what we've experienced with our sisters and brothers in savings groups around the world. The question for us has been, "Why?" Our initial impulse was to credit cultural or socioeconomic differences. In short, to write off their compelling community as isolated and inimitable. But through years of experience, observation, and interaction, we've realized we are far more similar than not. The practices that build community around the world apply here as well.

This book chronicles our journey of discovery and invites others to join us on that journey. We invite you to adopt a posture of curiosity along with us. Aloneness affects us more than we imagine, but we're learning from Jesus, the early church, and the global church what God intends for relationships and community.

We remain learners rather than experts, and we write from that posture. We don't have easy answers or perfect solutions! Because our journey toward creating and extending community continues, this book feels in some ways unfinished—yet we recognize that this is a message our world needs now, and we submit it to you, our readers, in the greatest humility.

We also recognize the limits of our perspectives, so we interviewed pastors across the United States and development practitioners around the world about trends they've witnessed: both those that bring joy and those that stir deep-seated concern. This book benefited tremendously from their wisdom.

Unprecedented numbers of people are experiencing aloneness and searching for something more. We've been saddened, even overwhelmed, as our awareness of the magnitude of the problem has grown. Yet we also share a sense of excitement and great hope because God has, in fact, created us for something more! We don't have to wait for social service organizations or government programs to address aloneness. Likewise, confronting this challenge is not the sole domain of medical or psychological experts. We believe that addressing an epidemic of loneliness is well within the sweet spot of our calling as Christ-followers.

Our hope and prayer is that as you read you will accept God's invitation and feel equipped and inspired to be part of a growing movement of creators and practitioners of the community God desires for us, as together, we find *the way back to one another.*

Part One

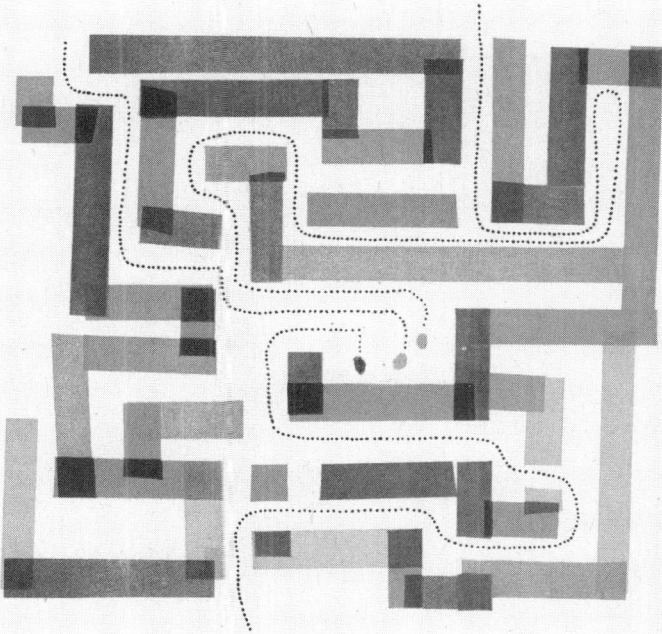

WE'VE LOST
OUR WAY

1

EYES OPEN
TO A BETTER WAY

It is not good for the man to be alone.

GENESIS 2:18

I (JEFF) RECEIVED JAKE'S NAME and address in 2020 from The Education and Employment Ministry (TEEM), an Oklahoma City–based nonprofit that prepares men and women for release from incarceration by providing employment and life skills training and establishing positive connections. Jake was my tenth mentee.

Normally I would visit mentees in prison and get to know them face-to-face, but because prisons were closed to visitors during the pandemic, Jake and I became old-fashioned pen pals. He was quick to write back when I reached out, and we got to know one another over a span of several months as he prepared to leave prison. Jake was winsome and engaging. He loved literature and learning, so I'd send a copy of books I was reading, and we'd discuss them in our letters, like an informal book club.

In one early letter, he spoke openly and with great clarity about the role of isolation in his past, present, and future. "I don't have any consistent contact with my family," he wrote. "I'm completely

and irrevocably isolated." He went on, "Having a pro-social relationship with anyone is new to me. Regardless, I want to attempt it."

In Jake's final letter, he informed me that he had been granted
early release for good behavior and would be transferred to another
facility across the state in preparation for release. Though long-
awaited, his taste of freedom was coming sooner than either one of
us had anticipated, and Jake was both hopeful and nervous about
what came next. I quickly penned a reply that included my contact
information so he could reach out after release, hoping he'd receive
it in time.

Several weeks went by without a word from Jake. I thought
perhaps his transfer had come before my letter arrived. Then one
day, he texted me. He'd been released the day before on the other
side of Oklahoma with only the clothes on his back and a few
dollars in his pocket. He was hoping to travel by bus to Oklahoma
City, where he could access TEEM's waiting resources. We arranged
transportation, and I had the privilege of meeting Jake for the first
time when I picked him up from the bus station.

The month that followed was filled with highs and lows. Jake
quickly found a job. He moved into safe housing, learned to navigate the bus system, and received some overdue medical attention.
We spent significant time together, and I heard more of his life story.
Jake's family had blown apart when he was a young child, and he
spent most of his formative years bouncing through the foster care
system. Jake couldn't recall a single long-term relationship, and he
often referred to the same sense of isolation he had referenced in
that early letter. In his early days of freedom, Jake was searching for
connection. Unfortunately, he found meth.

Despite many factors working in Jake's favor and a wealth of
natural talent and intelligence, he fell under the grip of addiction.
Jake stopped answering my calls and texts, and I learned that he

was living on the streets, adrift in an ocean of addiction and homelessness. I haven't managed to reach him since.

Researcher and journalist Johann Hari has argued, "The opposite of addiction isn't sobriety. It's connection."[1] The truth of Hari's assertion seemed so evident in Jake's example, as his words "irrevocably isolated" reverberated in my mind. Jake is a casualty of the loneliness epidemic. His example is among the more extreme outcomes of isolation, but it is nowhere near rare.

We're Lonely

We're lonely. Or at least half of us are.

According to multiple research studies, roughly half of Americans report that we are sometimes or always lonely, feeling left out, lacking companionship, or that no one knows us well.[2] When asked how close we felt to others emotionally, only 39 percent of us said we felt very connected.[3] But this is by no means an American problem alone. Based on a survey including 142 countries, over 2 billion people say they feel very or fairly lonely.[4]

We have fewer friends than we used to. In 1990, almost three-quarters of Americans had more than three close friends. By 2021, that number had dropped to 49 percent. Meanwhile, the percent of Americans who claim to have no close friends increased fourfold.[5] Fewer than half of us can affirm, "My relationships are as satisfying as I would want them to be."[6] Both the United Kingdom and Japan have established dedicated cabinet positions to address loneliness, indicating a growing recognition that loneliness is a public health issue warranting governmental intervention.[7]

Though the younger generation has been termed "the connected generation,"[8] it's a misnomer in all but the most superficial sense of the word. The rate of loneliness among younger generations is roughly 50 percent higher than that of those over age sixty.[9] Only one-third of those between the ages of eighteen and thirty-five indicate they "often feel deeply cared for by those around me."[10] Only 17 percent report feeling a deep social connection with others.[11]

We are lonely and getting lonelier.

Dire Impacts, Dire Implications

Loneliness has captured researchers' attention for decades. In 1939, Harvard University began what is today the longest continuous longitudinal study of human development. Over and again, the study has revealed and validated that "the strength of a person's connections with others can predict the health of both their body and their brain as they go through life."[12] In other words, healthy relationships contribute to a healthy body and mind, and the converse is also true.

More than three decades ago, in a groundbreaking essay which later became the book *Bowling Alone*, Robert Putnam prophetically sounded the alarm of our society's drift toward social disconnection and isolation.[13] Putnam made a striking observation about American identity: We're increasingly engaging solo in formerly social activities. To illustrate his point, Putnam cited a simultaneous increase in people bowling and decrease in bowling league participation. People were bowling alone. Putnam claimed that this shift weakened our national character and threatened our ability to build social connections.

In 2023, then–Surgeon General Vivek Murthy confirmed loneliness and isolation had reached dangerous levels in the United States, issuing an eighty-two-page advisory on the crisis. He warned that if we fail to build more connected lives and a more connected society, "We will pay an ever-increasing price in the form of our individual and collective health and well-being."[14] That price encompasses some of the most pressing problems our society faces: including substance abuse, incarceration, and homelessness, as Jake's story illustrates.

It also threatens our physical health. A meta-analysis (compilation of multiple studies) indicates that social isolation is as detrimental to our physical health as smoking fifteen cigarettes a day.[15] Insufficient social connection is also linked to a roughly 30 percent increased risk of heart disease and stroke.[16]

On the psychosocial front, social isolation and loneliness are primary risk factors for suicidal ideation and suicide. In the United States, suicide rates have climbed roughly 40 percent since 2000.[17] Similarly, loneliness is a direct contributor to depression, which has nearly doubled since 2015.[18]

It's not a pretty picture.

Researchers often draw a distinction between *social isolation* and *loneliness*, and it's helpful to understand the nuance.

Social isolation is the *objective* state of having few or no social relationships or experiencing inadequate meaningful social connectedness.[19] A socially isolated person doesn't get much interaction with other people—or maybe no interaction at all—and what interaction they may have doesn't lead to connection.

Loneliness is an *emotional* state of feeling alone or separated from others, marked by sadness, emptiness, and longing. It is the emotional response to the unmet need for meaningful relationships that provide connectedness, trust, reciprocity, and belonging. A lonely person feels disconnected, even if they regularly interact with other people and aren't physically isolated.

What About the Church?

We'd like to imagine that churchgoers fare better, with some (super) natural immunity against isolation and loneliness. After all, church affords myriad opportunities for consistent connection—yet the research doesn't bear that out:

- Fifty-four percent of both practicing Christians and non-Christians say they experience loneliness at least weekly, with 18 percent of practicing Christians (compared with 15 percent of non-Christians) indicating they are lonely all the time.[20]

- When practicing Christians between ages eighteen and thirty-five were asked what is missing from their church experience, the leading unmet need they expressed was friendships.[21]

- Another study (2022) found that our church leaders are not immune, with 65 percent of pastors indicating they often or sometimes feel lonely or isolated from others, an increase from 42 percent in 2015.[22]

"Christians are generally as lonely as non-Christians," summarizes Susan Mettes, author of *The Loneliness Epidemic*.[23] We agree. Our churches can be very lonely places, not just for those on the fringes.

Christianity Today editor-in-chief Russell Moore recounts a conversation with a middle-aged man who was very active in his church's activities. "I don't know how to say, 'I'm lonely,' without sounding like I'm saying, 'I'm a loser,' and I don't know how to say it without sounding like I'm an ungrateful Christian."[24]

Surrounded by Christian community, this man was expressing to Moore his longing for the "something more" that God created each one of us to crave. We recently spoke with a young couple whom we knew to be deeply committed to their faith and active in their church. After a decade of investment in their congregation—including serving as small group leaders and church board members—they were leaving their church. They weren't burned out or wrestling with theological differences, nor was there a crisis of faith. Rather, they explained that despite all their service and activity, they felt deeply disconnected. They knew most fellow congregants by name, and they had warm conversations during Sunday morning greeting time. But that was all. Relationships remained shallow and superficial, and they couldn't escape the feeling that no one truly knew them (or wanted to), nor did they truly know others despite their longing.

They weren't exactly isolated or lonely, but they craved deeper, more meaningful relationships and struggled to find others who shared not only the longing but also the commitment to pursuing true community. For them, the relational deficit far outweighed the church's preaching, teaching, events, activities, and programs. After ten years, and with great sadness, they left their church.

The experiences of the middle-aged man, the young couple, and so many like them point to a spiritual component to this phenomenon that neither the term *isolation* nor *loneliness* captures. Throughout our writing, we'll use the term *aloneness* to refer to this broader reality. *Aloneness* is the absence of interdependent relationships God designed us to experience. We'll unpack this definition at length in the chapters to come, but in brief, we believe that many who are not objectively isolated and may not describe themselves as lonely are still not experiencing God's rich design for relationships. God said it isn't good to be alone—yet so many of us are.

Perhaps even more than loneliness and isolation, our aloneness can go unnoticed by others and even by ourselves. Fundamentally, we may not know what we're missing. We (Jeff and Phil) couldn't articulate our desire for something richer and deeper in our relationships until we observed a better way among the savings groups. We needed to see that what we'd accepted as normal was neither God's design nor his best for our lives. Our most compelling glimpses of God's beautiful design for community came as we spent time outside our home culture where we were exposed and awakened to something immeasurably better than our former vision of community. Our discontent or vague dissatisfaction points to a different, better design for community.

In the almost two decades that I (Jeff) have spent overseeing small groups for Life.Church, a multicampus church in the United States, I've had a front-row seat to a dramatic increase in aloneness. I've seen how this challenge impacts our churches and our congregants, sometimes without their conscious recognition. It's not because church leaders aren't creating the opportunity to build relationships. But too often it eludes us. Church leaders across the country confirm this problem is far-reaching and severe in their communities and congregations alike.

Driven by our interest in this topic, we scheduled conversations with pastors from Denver to Dallas to Philadelphia to gain their input. We wanted to know if the rather discouraging statistics on loneliness and isolation—and our observations on the unstudied phenomenon of aloneness—represented their experiences as pastors in their communities. While each shared bright spots where people were experiencing community, their overwhelming response was, "Yes, lack of connection is a huge problem within our church, just like it is in our broader community!"

Stephen pastors a church in a walkable neighborhood near downtown Fort Worth, Texas. Packed with condos and lofts mixed with shops, bars, and restaurants, the area seems to be designed for community, yet Pastor Stephen sees hints that people—including those who attend his church—are alone. "Everybody is connected digitally but not emotionally or personally. Everything can look great on the outside, but there's not a depth of relationship that people are experiencing."[25]

In fact, when Pastor Stephen surveyed his church on their top stressors in life, the number one answer, given by 28 percent of respondents, was their relationships—or lack thereof.

Ryan, who serves as executive pastor at a church in West Philadelphia, shared that his congregation includes many college students and young families. "Many are high-performing, overscheduled students and young professionals who work a lot," Pastor Ryan explained.[26] Many of these young professionals are second- and third-generation Korean immigrants whose tradition and culture profoundly value community. But even with that influence, congregants struggle to connect due to the pace of their lives.

Coming to Grips

We've been awakened to the growing loneliness and aloneness in our communities and churches. From the scourge of addictions that attempt to fill the void in relationships; to our rapidly growing reliance on social media as an arms-length alternative to face-to-face relationships; to the proliferation of streaming services that keep us tethered to our screens; to the rise in medications for depression and long waiting lists for counseling services, the signs are there.

Equally concerning are the aloneness and loneliness that we don't see. One out of every two people we work with, pass in the aisles of the grocery store, or sit next to in church on Sunday would say in one form or another, "I'm lonely." Yet our aloneness, our longing for deeper, more meaningful relationships and a safe and accepting community of friends isn't something we're likely to lead with in our conversations.

We're culturally conditioned to "put our best foot forward." As singer/songwriter Wayne Watson put it in his song "Friend of a Wounded Heart," "Smile, make 'em think you're happy. Lie, and say that things are fine. And hide that empty longing that you feel. Don't ever show it, just keep your heart concealed."[27] Whether secular or Christian, powerful cultural conditioning works against admitting—and solving—the problem of aloneness. We know people who are lonely or alone, probably lots of them. The paradox is that often we don't know that we know them, as their aloneness remains undetected and loneliness unshared.

Coming to grips with this bleak and veiled landscape has been a difficult journey for us. As we said earlier, it's not a pretty picture. Yet as stark as that reality may seem, in our experience, conversations, interviews, and research, we've also witnessed the depths of God's transformation. We've seen examples here in the United States and around the world of aloneness replaced by joyful belonging as a result of God's work in and through followers of Jesus. We've seen people rediscovering God's beautiful design for relationships and community. We've learned from the successes of the global church in creating these contagious communities that are not only welcoming the lonely but eradicating aloneness. In spite of the bleak landscape we've described, we have ample reason to "take heart" (John 16:33).

A Call to Something Immeasurably Better

If you're currently more alone than you'd like to be, we recognize you may be starting this book and this journey from a place of pain rather than conviction, and we applaud your courage in taking this initial step. (If you are in a state of crisis, we urge you to put the book down now and reach out to someone to share what is happening in your life: a pastor, counselor, friend, doctor, or anyone you trust to offer encouragement and partnership as you move forward. You can also dial 988 to reach a caring counselor free of charge, anytime day or night.)

Or it could be that you're experiencing meaningful relational connections and community and feel drawn to come alongside others who are not, to help them experience the same. That could take place at work or in your home, neighborhood, or church. In effect, you want to be a catalyst of relationships and community as God intended.

Or perhaps you haven't thought of yourself as being lonely, yet you recognize that your own relationships aren't as deep and fulfilling as you wish they were. We're with you.

We have found ourselves straddling each of these categories in different seasons of life. We've experienced periods of loneliness. In my early adulthood, I (Jeff) at times felt embarrassed that I didn't have any close friends, even though I was on a pastoral staff and spent my days surrounded by people. Later, I wrestled with crushing doubts about whether I'd be accepted as a trustworthy person (a story I'll share in chapter four).

Particularly in two of our frequent relocations, Becca and I (Phil) experienced the gaping void and prolonged, gnawing loneliness and isolation of leaving family and close friends behind, of being "friend-less." As I will share in a later chapter, an especially dark season left me not only in physical peril but also in a state of utter despair. By God's grace and the intervention of a couple who showed me I was not alone, I am penning these words today.

Even now we find ourselves in the tension of longing to experience deeper, more meaningful connections and create safe havens for others, yet struggling to find time for dinner with friends or relationship-building with neighbors. Our journey to trade our aloneness for the community God intends continues.

Wherever you're coming from, this book is written to encourage you to create and experience the relationships and community God envisioned, starting where you are today. Think for a moment about how many people you interact with each day: family, neighbors, and coworkers as well as people you encounter while shopping, recreating, or attending church. For many of us, it adds up to a lot of interactions. As we work through the chapters in this book, we'll point out specific ways you can approach these daily interactions with greater awareness and clarified intention. Every one of us can contribute to solving this problem.

Most importantly, we believe Christ's followers—his body, the church—are best positioned to respond to the crisis of aloneness. In fact, the church has a long history of stepping into moments of crisis with compassion and courage.

In AD 260, at the height of a deadly plague, the people of Carthage, a major city in the Roman Empire, fled for their own protection, leaving their sick and dying behind. While most rushed *from* the infected city, early Christians, in contrast, rushed in, caring for those who had been left behind. They became first responders to the epidemic, taking the biblical call to love one another so seriously that many sacrificed their lives to fulfill it. Historian Rodney Stark writes that their countercultural response catalyzed the spread of Christianity.[28]

We live in a very different context today. Many in our society are familiar with Christianity, but far fewer see its relevance to their lives. They don't see God's body, the church—*us* living in community—offering hope amid the challenges of our day. But we believe they would if we, like our ancestors in the faith, became first responders to the epidemic of our era.

The Surgeon General's report on the loneliness epidemic makes scant mention of the church as a solution, in a subset of a section targeting community-based organizations: a seeming afterthought. We beg to differ! Addressing the loneliness epidemic and our broader crisis of aloneness should not be outsourced to government social service agencies or community organizations. It is not to be relinquished to "the experts" like professional counselors, therapists, or even our church staff. While each of these individuals and groups has an important role to play, we believe they are secondary. It is *our* primary calling—yours and mine as followers of Jesus—to create and be part of something that is immeasurably better than our current personal and cultural experience.

We'll spend the next chapter diving deep into God's design for relationships and community. In chapters three through seven we'll jump into the postural and practical shifts we'll need to make to pursue the way back to one another, rediscovering how to live as people created for community.

Jesus' invitation to another way beckons. We want more for our neighborhoods, workplaces, churches, families, and ourselves— and if you do too, we hope you'll join us on this journey to discover how to live as people created for community, finding in the serious challenge of the loneliness epidemic a compelling opportunity to create and experience the kind of connection God has always intended for us.

Reflection Questions

We firmly believe that individuals can take many steps to address aloneness and even become catalysts of community, but we also recognize that, by definition, relationships and community require others. At the end of each chapter, we've included reflection questions to help you consider steps that you can take on your own, as well as discussion questions to facilitate conversation among a small group of friends or fellow believers. We're confident that reading, discussing, and practicing these principles together in a small group setting will enrich the experience.

Reflect Individually

- Where do you notice increasing aloneness in our society? Where do you see signs of aloneness in your own life and the lives of those around you?

- How satisfied are you with your relationships? What, if anything, is missing?

- To what degree do you feel you are fully experiencing the relationships God designed us to experience?

- Describe the connection you feel to others in your church. What contributes to that feeling?

- What small, intentional efforts can you make this week to get to know someone around you better?

Discuss Together

- What can we do together to increase our awareness of the people around us who might be experiencing aloneness?

- The US Surgeon General's report on loneliness gave little focus to the church as a potential solution. Why do you think that is? What role can the church play in addressing loneliness and aloneness?

- What factors might contribute to feelings of aloneness felt by people within our church?

- (For the brave!) When you think about our group, what changes could we make to cultivate the deep, meaningful relationships God intends for us?

2

IT'S AS SIMPLE AND AS HARD AS THAT

Your love for one another will prove to the world that you are my disciples.

JOHN 13:35 NLT

SEVERAL YEARS AGO, I (PHIL) GATHERED with a Rwandan savings group for their weekly meeting. We sat under the shade of a towering tree next to one member's mud brick home. The group had been meeting weekly over the past few years to save and invest together, and it was obvious that they had become personal and collective entrepreneurs. With a foundational commitment to God and each other, their meetings included time studying God's Word, praying, and worshiping as well as fellowshipping. Perhaps most striking to me from the outset, they were "doing life together," both during their meetings and in the hours and days in between.

Their care and generosity was compelling and extended beyond their savings group, as they paid school fees for orphaned children, firm in their resolve that no child in their community would be deprived of education. This was a small group with an outsized impact, and when I visited they were eager to share what had changed in their lives since joining the group.

But before sharing, they focused their attention on caring for two members absent from that day's meeting due to illness. They arranged to use their own resources to buy food and other necessities for the two women and their families. There was no debate about whether to help, though this generosity obviously represented a sacrifice for the gathered members who relied on their daily labor for their daily bread.

In addition to their financial generosity, group members would sacrifice their time, delivering the goods, providing whatever assistance might be needed around the members' homes, and sitting with and praying over their ill friends. When the leader asked for volunteers, hands shot up around the circle. There was not even a hint of the imposition or inconvenience I imagined I might feel under similar circumstances.

As we moved on to testimonies, one group member after the next talked about businesses launched, assets acquired, basic health insurance procured, their own children provided for, and school scholarships donated to children outside their group. Members clapped and cheered each story of transformation, and an air of celebration pervaded the entire meeting.

Then an older woman, perhaps the group's matriarch, stood up to share. Whether out of respect or in anticipation of words of wisdom, the boisterous group immediately quieted. Her eyes connected with each friend around the circle as she spoke softly, lovingly, and with great resolve. "We have so much to thank God for," she said. "But do not forget that before our group started, we were isolated. We stayed alone in our houses. We were forgotten in our community. It was as if we were invisible." She paused for emphasis. "We thought that even God had forgotten about us."

Heads nodded, affirming the truth of her words.

"But God provided this group for us, and now we know he loves us. And we love each other. We are like a family. If anyone ever tried to separate us, we would not let them." For a few seconds after the matriarch finished talking, the hush lingered. Then loud applause and amens erupted from the assembly. Moments later, the group broke into song and dance.

The group's love and impact on both its members and the broader community captivated me, but it was the matriarch's words that I revisited for months to come: "God provided this group for us, and now we know he loves us. And we love each other." What was the connection between experiencing the love of a community and the love of God? This comment surpassed simple, deeply held gratitude to God for new-found friends. It seemed that these sisters and brothers experienced God and his love through each other. They embodied 1 John 4:12, which says, "No one has ever seen God; but if we love one another, God lives in us and his love is made complete in us."

In his book *Life Together*, theologian Dietrich Bonhoeffer writes, "Christ became our Brother in order to help us. Through him our brother has become Christ for us in the power and authority of the commission Christ has given to him."[1] We experience God through our sisters and brothers, embodying the very presence of God in each act of humility, service, burden-bearing, confession, or listening directed toward others. We are created for, and experience God in, community grounded in Christ.

Relational Foundation

In the first days of creation, God made earth and sky, oceans and land, plants and animals. Then he said, "Let us make mankind in our image, in our likeness" (Genesis 1:26), and he made the first human being, Adam. If we gloss over these familiar words, we miss the foundational truth that God shared about his nature—and ours—in the very first chapter of the Bible.

In choosing the words "us" and "our," rather than "me" and "my," God is speaking of his relational nature. He is a single being, comprising three: Father, Son, and Spirit. We aren't wise enough to explain or understand the Trinity, yet it's a great and mysterious foundation of our faith that God, in his very being, is relational.[2] We know from the opening words of Scripture that God is relational, so we too—made in his image—are relational. Put simply, we were created for relationships. Author and pastor Rev. Irwyn Ince writes, "For humanity to be the image of God, it must embody beautiful community."[3]

In the creation narrative, our triune God commends each day's work with the words, "It is good." The first time he declares otherwise is in Genesis 2:18, when God says, "It is *not good* for the man to be alone" (emphasis added). "Aloneness"—not sin—was the first problem to beset the first person: Then and now, it is not good to be alone.

God's response to Adam's aloneness is to make "a helper suitable for him." The word our English translation renders "helper" is the Hebrew word *ezer* (pronounced *ay'-zer*).[4] The translation has caused a lot of debate, as modern readers ponder the subservience of this "helper." Many understand the term to mean "servant" or "junior assistant" and even extrapolate gender roles and marital responsibilities from its use, but this is an inaccurate interpretation. In Scripture, the majority of uses of the word *ezer* are in direct reference to God, as helper and protector. For example, Psalm 121:1-2 says, "I lift up my eyes to the mountains—where does my help [*ezer*] come from? My help [*ezer*] comes from the LORD, the Maker of heaven and earth." Through the prophet Hosea, God even refers to himself as an *ezer*: "You are destroyed, Israel, because you are against me, against your helper [*ezer*]" (Hosea 13:9). Clearly, subservience is not the intent of *ezer*, so what does it mean?

In addition to the word *help* or *helper*, the closest English translation for *ezer* might be the Shakespearean-sounding word *succor*. It means "assistance and support in times of hardship and distress," a word derived from the Latin *succurrere*, which means "to run to help."[5]

In the garden, what brings Adam out of his state of aloneness isn't just someone who can help him name animals or harvest fruit. It isn't a person with whom he can chat idly about the weather or exchange hellos in passing. It's an *ezer*: an ally who can run to his aid. A companion who will walk with him as he walks with God, someone who will help him be the human God intended him to be.

The women and men who were members of the savings group I (Phil) met in Rwanda were delivering daily necessities to ill members and paying school fees for orphans in their community, beautifully embodying the concept of *ezer*. Group members eagerly responded to care for practical and relational needs, undeterred by busy schedules, the threat of catching what could have been a contagious illness, or the impulse to care exclusively for their own. Rather than shying away, they ran to the rescue. They were *ezers*.

To be created in God's image means to be called as an *ezer* to other image bearers: a loving companion, someone who sees and responds to others' needs, an ally who runs to the rescue.

Love One Another

The relational call doesn't end with *ezer* in the Old Testament. In fact, as powerful as the meaning and implications of *ezer* are, it is just the beginning. We can be an *ezer* (one who helps, runs to the rescue) to those we know well, like the fellow savings group members, or even to those previously unknown to us, like orphaned children in the community. *Ezer* can exist outside an ongoing relationship, but the relational call grows deeper and stronger with the introduction in the New Testament of the Greek term *allēlōn* (pronounced *a-lay'-lone*).

Allēlōn, which is translated "one another," conveys mutuality, coparticipation, and relationship. In each of the forty-seven instances where it shows up in the New Testament to offer instruction,[6] *allēlōn* conveys how two or more *ezers* might interact: how we might run to one another's aid in a way that overcomes aloneness. We have continually seen this dynamic at work within savings groups, with members both giving and receiving in reciprocal relationships.

Perhaps the most well-known *allēlōn* verses are John 13:34-35. Jesus offered these instructions to his disciples gathered for the Last Supper: "A new command I give you: Love one another (*allēlōn*). As I have loved you, so you must love one another (*allēlōn*). By this everyone will know that you are my disciples, if you love one another (*allēlōn*)." These were Jesus' parting words to his closest followers. Knowing that he would be crucified the next day, Jesus would have chosen this particular counsel with great intentionality, wanting to sear this message into their minds.

Loving one another was not an optional add-on for Jesus' disciples to consider. Jesus called it a command. In his last evening with his disciples, Jesus reminded his followers how to live as citizens of an upside-down kingdom: Love one another as I have loved you.

Jesus referred to this command as "new," emphasizing how it differed from the familiar Old Testament directive to "love your neighbor as yourself" (Leviticus 19:18). His love was radically countercultural—marked by humility, sacrifice, and servanthood. Jesus' way of living and loving was indeed new, not just fulfilling the law but transcending it. So much of what he taught and demonstrated regarding relationships ran counter to Jewish tradition and the culture of the day. Rather than the accepted and expected Jewish teaching of an eye for an eye or a tooth for a tooth, Jesus said turn the other cheek (Matthew 5:38-39). Rather than loving neighbors and hating enemies, Jesus said, "Love your enemies and pray for those who persecute you" (Matthew 5:44). Rather than repaying evil for evil, Jesus was about to lay down his life for the sins of those who would mock him, beat him, reject him, or live in persistent apathy toward him. Jesus modeled a new culture, and although his disciples adopted it imperfectly, their countercultural others-focused posture would be the mark of discipleship—and the method of lighting this message on fire.

Each to All

Jesus delivered his "love one another" command not to each disciple individually but to the disciples as a whole. This instruction was meant to guide their life together, and in Acts 2, we find a new word to describe the fellowship of believers living in obedience to this "love one another" command. Luke calls it *koinōnia* (koy-nohn-ee'-ah). Theologians have unpacked the meaning of *koinōnia* over the centuries, providing varying definitions—including community, fellowship, joint participation, sharing, and intimacy. The experience defies simple description. At its most basic level, *koinōnia* is what happens when *allēlōn* love is applied within a group. It isn't just the fulfillment of God's relational intent one to another (*ezer*) or to each other one-on-one (*allēlōn*) but each to all—many *allēlōn*s simultaneously. And it is something to behold!

EZER
"One to Another"

ALLĒLŌN
"To Each Other"

KOINŌNIA
"Each to All"

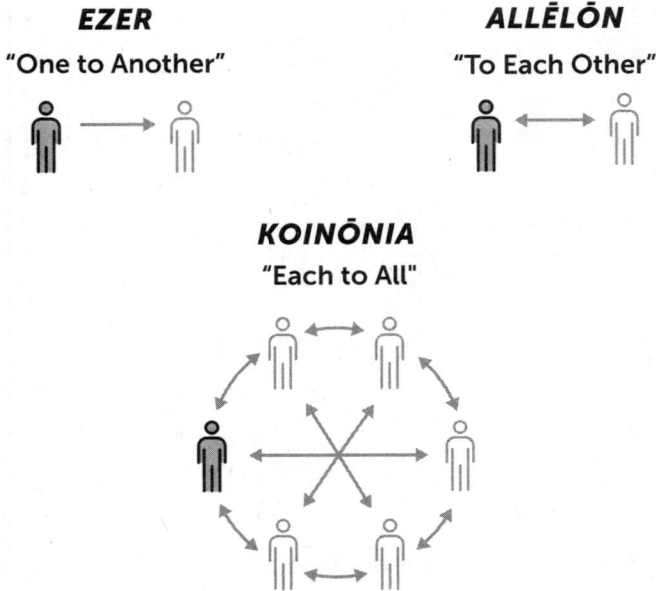

Acts 2:42-47 paints a picture of a vibrant experience of togetherness.

> [The believers] devoted themselves to the apostles' teaching and to fellowship, to the breaking of bread and to prayer. Everyone was filled with awe at the many wonders and signs performed by the apostles. All the believers were together and had everything in common. They sold property and possessions to give to anyone who had need. Every day they continued to meet together in the temple courts. They broke bread in their homes and ate together with glad and sincere hearts, praising God and enjoying the favor of all the people. And the Lord added to their number daily those who were being saved.

In Acts 4:32, Luke adds that those who believed were "one in heart and mind." Luke illustrates *koinōnia* by painting a picture of a church characterized by unity, generosity, service, and magnetism.

When we've visited savings groups and come away captivated, it's because we have seen *koinōnia* among their members. We've caught a vision of what God intended—for all of us! As we've learned from these *koinōnia* communities, we've begun to believe that Scripture identified the answer to our modern loneliness epidemic over two thousand years ago: It's as simple and as hard as *koinōnia*.

The Gift of *Koinōnia*

Koinōnia is a simple solution because it's been there all along, right under our noses in the pages of the Bible. It won't take an influx of material resources, vast infrastructure, or a PhD to understand and implement. But *koinōnia* is also hard, because we're powerless to manufacture it. (Otherwise companies would be marketing and distributing *koinōnia* far and wide as the cure for what ails half of us!) As theologian Eberhard Arnold identified, "The community we seek . . . is fed by divine strength and comes to true unity in God not by reason of our own strength, or even our collective strength, but through a power given from above."[7]

Once created, we are equally powerless to sustain this others-focused way of living in our own strength. Its creation and continuance come from God, even while we can and must make postural and practical shifts that allow us to receive this gift.

Rather than a program to implement, *koinōnia* is a way of life, encompassing these common characteristics:

- **Shared identity:** Our common identity is in and through Jesus Christ, brothers and sisters in God's family, none of us perfect, yet each filled with gratitude for his extravagant grace and unconditional love

- **Shared purpose:** Committed to the practice of *allēlōn* and *ezer* together as a family; to loving and serving God, each other, and those in the greater community

- **Shared experience:** Intentional about gathering, spending time with each other, doing life together, and experiencing together our shared identity and purpose

In *koinōnia* communities, as the savings group matriarch rightly recognized, we experience the love of Christ through others.

Experienced Through Others

Several years ago my wife, Christy, and I (Jeff) were about to head to work for the day when our phones buzzed with a text message our friend Margaret sent to our entire church small group. She and her husband of five years, Josiah, were expecting their first baby any day. But this was not a happy message about a baby on the way. Josiah had collapsed into unconsciousness on their kitchen floor. The paramedics arrived, could not revive him, and rushed Josiah and Margaret to the hospital.

We rushed after them. Josiah didn't make it (we later found out his heart simply stopped due to an undetected defect). When we arrived, our small group sat with Margaret in a private waiting room in silent shock. It was one of the most heartbreaking experiences of my life. Margaret was nine months pregnant, and she'd lost the love of her life and the father of her little girl. She delivered their daughter, Linley, the next day.

A few months before Josiah's unexpected death, he'd struck up a conversation with a man named Dale at church one Sunday morning. Josiah didn't know that this was the first Sunday Dale had attended church in many years or that Dale had come at the coaxing of friends and his fiancée, Andrea. But as a result of their conversation and Josiah's invitation, Dale and Andrea joined our group of friends.

A few weeks after that initial meeting, during one of our small group meetings, Dale shared with us that he was beginning to understand the gospel but was not yet ready to choose to follow Jesus. We asked Dale, "How can we be most helpful to you right now?"

He responded, "You're already doing everything you need to do by letting me be here." He went on to say, "I feel some kind of peace when I'm here with you all." Now, in the wake of Josiah's death, Dale was plunged into grief alongside us as we mourned Josiah and focused on being a friend to Margaret.

In the months to come, the road was not easy, but I watched the power of relationships and community play out as our group of friends, alongside Margaret's out-of-state family, cared for her and stood with one another. The first year was filled with all the tension, anger, confusion, sadness, conflict, and disappointment you might expect around a tragedy like this one. It was messy in every way, but our group hung together.

Throughout the year, Dale shared a lot about his life story. I always admired how authentic and transparent Dale was with us; he risked a lot with his honesty, and although he was new to our group, he and Andrea embraced Margaret and Linley as family.

Together, over time, we saw hope and new life emerge out of the pain. Linley has grown into a beautiful young lady, and Margaret has remarried and is experiencing the joy of a young family once again. In time, Dale chose to follow Jesus, and I was honored to baptize him, with our small group bearing witness. He's a committed follower of Jesus today. He and Andrea are married and have two amazing little boys. And I think of the Rwandan matriarch's words: "God provided this group for us, and now we know he loves us. And we love each other."

One Another Instructions

At first glance, "love one another" seems a simple enough instruction to comprehend, if not a difficult one to follow. In the earliest days of Christianity, those who received that command walked closely with Jesus himself. When he decreed "love as I have loved," specific memories and interactions almost certainly came to mind. But soon the gospel spread. First to 120 believers (Acts 1:15), then to more than 3,000 (Acts 2:41), "and the Lord added to their number daily" (Acts 2:47).

Outside the epicenter of Jerusalem, the gospel advanced as new believers returned home and others embarked on missionary journeys, faithful to Jesus' call to "make disciples of all nations" (Matthew 28:19). These new converts lacked the benefit of rubbing shoulders with Jesus while he walked the earth. They couldn't call on personal experience to know what his love had looked like.

Roughly half of our New Testament is attributed to the apostle Paul, and much of his writing took the form of letters to these believers in the early Christian world. In Paul's letters, he added clarity to how those who wanted to walk in the way of Jesus should love one another.

In letters contextualized to his recipients, addressing both sound doctrine and godly living, he spoke to challenges they were facing and offered encouragement. To the ethnically diverse church in Rome, Paul wrote "accept one another" (Romans 15:7). To the church in Ephesus, which was beset by "fables" (1 Timothy 1:4 KJV), Paul instructed, "Speak the truth in love" to one another (Ephesians 4:15 NLT). To the church in Galatia, whose insistence on submission to Mosaic law for new believers resulted in division within their ranks, Paul cautioned they must not "bite and devour" one another but should instead "serve one another humbly in love" (Galatians 5:13, 15). Rather than finger-pointing and condemning those they believed to be wrong, Paul said they must "carry each other's burdens," writing, "in this way you will fulfill the law of Christ" (Galatians 6:2): the law of love.

Additional one-another instructions included:

- Be kind and compassionate to one another. (Ephesians 4:32)

- Bear with and forgive one another. (Colossians 3:13)

- Strive to do what is good for one another, and don't repay wrong for wrong (1 Thessalonians 5:15)

- Be devoted to one another in love. (Romans 12:10)

- Consider one another as more important than yourselves. (Philippians 2:3 NASB)

- Encourage (or comfort) one another. (1 Thessalonians 4:18; 5:11)

These were messages that each group of recipients needed to hear. Each gave greater clarity and form to Jesus' "love one another" command. As we read these letters that were written *for* us but not *to* us, they remain truth-filled and God-inspired. But we acknowledge that some of our context has changed since Paul penned these letters. For instance, greeting one another with a holy kiss (Romans 16:16; 1 Corinthians 16:20; 2 Corinthians 13:12; 1 Thessalonians 5:26) might not fly in the United States today (though perhaps in many other cultures it still could!). Obviously there are also lifestyle and technological changes that Paul wouldn't have accounted for in his letters. So what might it look like to live out *ezer, allēlōn,* and *koinōnia* today, particularly in light of the growing epidemic of loneliness and the associated impacts we've shared?

One-Anothers for Today's Church

We've pondered all this and wondered, if Paul were writing to the church in the United States today, what one-anothers would he emphasize? What aspects of our culture (both "Christian" and secular) would he address, and how would he encourage us to love one another in the countercultural way of Jesus? Once again we were guided by our sisters and brothers in the global church as we visited savings groups around the world.

We've seen savings group members transcending their cultural context to embrace the culture of Christ's kingdom—and their practices looked very similar, whether they were living in Haiti, Rwanda, or Peru. As we sat at the feet of these Christ-centered communities—practitioners of *ezer*, *allēlōn*, and *koinōnia*—and learned from them, we were filled with hope that we, too, can overcome aloneness together. What we saw in these savings groups not only piqued our curiosity and inspired us but also revealed some postural and practical shifts we must make—some contextualized one-anothers—to become a people known for our love not our loneliness.

These are not new (unbiblical) inventions. Rather, they are a contemporary articulation of what we suspect Paul and the New Testament writers might call out within our context.

- **Depend on one another**: Where we've witnessed true *koinōnia*, it has been among communities that embrace interdependence—both in mindset and in practice—consistently prioritizing "we" over "me."

- **Know one another**: Members feel safe with and loved by one another. Even with faults in full view, they know they belong. The safety they experience in these relationships allows them to become remarkably open and vulnerable with one another.

- **Talk with one another**: Members gather, share, talk, and listen to each other well beyond the bounds of prescribed or customary interactions. They take the time to understand one another.

- **Welcome one another**: These communities are simultaneously close-knit and welcoming. They see themselves as people who have been welcomed in, and, in gratitude, they are quick to welcome others.

- **Commit to one another**: *Koinōnia* communities model deep relational commitment and tenacity, actively serving, encouraging, and caring for their sisters and brothers.

Why these five? First, we found that many of the scriptural "one-anothers" are embedded in each of these five concepts. For example, committing to one another produces the fruit of helping one another and bearing one another's burdens. Second, from interviews, observations, and statistics, we can see that each of these areas is lacking in our current cultural climate, and we believe each is a vital step on the path back to one another.

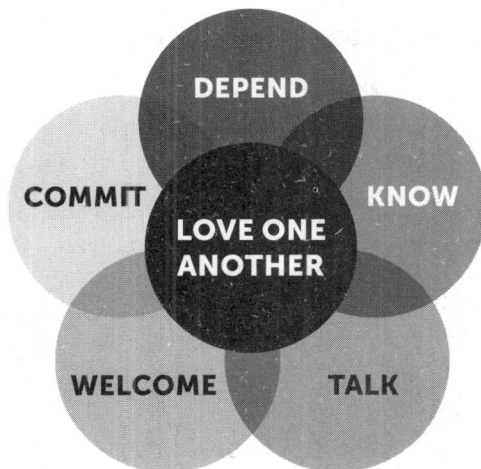

Each of these "ingredients" is a key part of God's recipe for community. While living in Africa, I (Phil) savored Rwandan ginger tea: a mixture of milk, sugar, fresh ginger, and black tea leaves harvested nearby. While each of those ingredients may be appreciated in its own right, they only make Rwandan ginger tea when combined.

Remove one of the ingredients and the finished product is something less than what it's meant to be.

The whole is more than the sum of its parts. Moreover, once combined, the ingredients can no longer be separated. So it is with these one-anothers. Each "ingredient" of community permeates the others. Interdependence breeds commitment, and talking to one another allows us to know and be known by others. This relational richness and security encourages a welcoming posture, inviting others to experience what we're experiencing. While each one-another may be viewed separately as a vital ingredient in our Christ-centered communities, they become exponentially more beautiful as they permeate and enrich the others.

By taking small, intentional steps toward embracing and integrating these one-another ingredients, we will, like our global teachers, become people who experience and foster deep and loving relationships and community.

We wish we could invite each one of you to see *ezer*, *allēlōn*, and *koinōnia* as we've seen it embraced in communities around the world. But perhaps there's a still-better invitation we can extend: Be a part of creating it in your own community. God's design for relationships and community—*ezer*, *allēlōn*, and *koinōnia*—offers the antidote to the loneliness epidemic, and it's available to each of us as we obey Christ's command to love one another. It's as simple and as hard as that.

Reflect Individually

- Who are the *ezer*s in your life who would run to your rescue? In what ways are you an *ezer* to others? How do you look for opportunities to help a friend or stranger?

- In John 13:34, Jesus called loving one another a "new" commandment. What was new about the way Jesus loved others? How does he invite you to make your love for others new?

- What does practicing *allēlōn* look like in your life? How do you show love to your friends? How could you grow in your love for each other?

- How could you better support those around you, given your resources and gifts?

- How does culture pull you away from *ezer*, *allēlōn*, and *koinōnia*? How could you resist those currents?

Discuss Together

- Consider how savings groups and the early church exemplified *koinōnia*. In what ways did these groups love one another? What similarities and differences do you notice between their practice of loving one another and how we love one another?

- What are some biblical examples of the Father, Son, and Holy Spirit being in community together? How could we apply these examples to our relationships?

- How can we become a people known for our love, not our loneliness?

Part Two

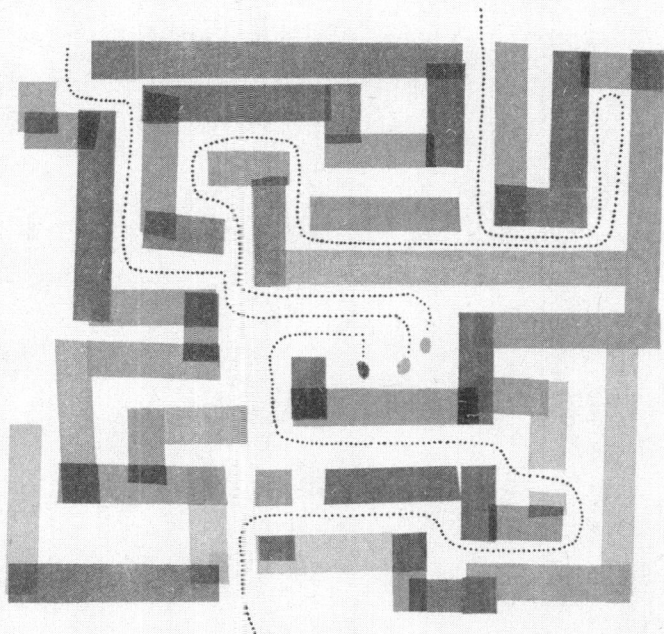

ONE-ANOTHERS
FOR THE AMERICAN
CHURCH

3

DEPEND ON ONE ANOTHER

For by the grace given me I say to every one of you: Do not think of yourself more highly than you ought, but rather think of yourself with sober judgment, in accordance with the faith God has distributed to each of you. For just as each of us has one body with many members, and these members do not all have the same function, so in Christ we, though many, form one body, and each member belongs to all the others.

ROMANS 12:3-5

I (JEFF) HAD BEEN IN A NEW ROLE on the Life.Church team only a month when my then-boss, Kevin, put his finger on a growth challenge that's been with me all of my adult life. As I transitioned from a role on one of Life.Church's many campuses to overseeing community and missions across all campuses, I asked Kevin to give me a few weeks to understand the current state of missions and small groups churchwide. Before developing a vision for the future, I wanted to ensure I fully grasped our starting point. With Kevin's blessing, I launched an informal listening campaign to capture perspectives and ideas across the organization.

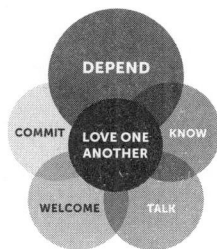

A few weeks later, Kevin invited the church leadership team to hear my proposal for the next season of LifeGroups and missions at Life.Church. I needed this group's buy-in to proceed, so a lot was riding on the meeting. It seemed to be going well, with enthusiastic head nods and affirmations around the table, but I couldn't help noticing Kevin quietly jotting notes on a tiny yellow sticky pad as I spoke.

After I finished sharing, the leadership team confirmed their enthusiasm for what I proposed. They were engaged and excited, and their support energized me. Everyone filed out of the conference room until just Kevin and I remained. When we were alone, Kevin held up the sticky note, covered in several dozen tally marks. "Do you know what I was counting?" he asked. I had no idea. "These are the times you said 'I' or 'me' when you should have said 'we' or 'us.'" Kevin let that truth sink in before continuing. "If you think for a minute that you can accomplish what you envision with your effort, it'll never happen. This vision will only happen if we all go together in an integrated way."

If the problem had been my words alone, this would have been an easy fix. But from the moment Kevin pointed out this trend in my language, I recognized it was symptomatic of a broader problem: My overgrown sense of independence made me feel I had to be the one with all the answers. Sometimes it still does, as diagnosing the problem has proven easier than overcoming it.

Independence Is Our Default Setting

Aspects of our personalities and life experiences undoubtedly contribute to our overemphasis on independence, but in many ways, this is an American challenge. While independence is seen as a cultural touchstone throughout the global West, Americans can take it to extremes. Nowhere does the value of independence shine brighter than it does here in the United States. Independence Day is one of our nation's most popular holidays. The "Don't Tread on Me" flag, which has its roots in Revolutionary America, has surged in popularity in the twenty-first century as a symbol of the American ethos of independence. We treasure our independence, pursue it, and elevate it as an ultimate good. From 2017 to 2021, the percent of Americans who went so far as to mention "freedom, independence, and their ability to do what they want to do" *as a source of meaning in life* nearly doubled.[1]

As Americans, we consider ourselves separate from others and in control of our individual destiny. The formative stories impressed upon us and passed on to our children are of those who broke the mold, carving new paths for themselves and all of us: revolutionaries, pioneers, and explorers. American cultural heroes tend to rise above the crowd and accomplish something independently. For example, the debate over the greatest basketball player of all time—Michael Jordan or LeBron James—is a much hotter topic than any debate over the most outstanding team. We collectively idolize corporate leaders like Steve Jobs, Bill Gates, and Jeff Bezos but seldom speak of the teams of thousands that supported and enabled their success.

We even display our idolization of independence in our greetings. When introducing ourselves to others, we often mention things we're proud of, such as our profession or where we live. Meanwhile, in the global East, introductions emphasize a sense of relational belonging and interdependence: "I'm the father of Riku" in Japan, or "I'm the son of Ravi" in India. These greetings may feel like small, inconsequential things, but they subtly reflect what our cultures value.

In the United States, we see ourselves as paragons of independence and protagonists of our own stories, free to pursue our careers, express our opinions, select our leaders, raise our children how we see fit, and live the lives we deem worth pursuing. We don't see how this normalized sense of overgrown independence is an anomaly, both geographically and historically. For most of history, people lived in much closer community than we experience today. Families lived in clans, and groups relied on each other in a highly interdependent manner. The concept of moving from city to city in pursuit of career aspirations, not knowing and depending on the neighbors next door or across the street (and not having time to get to know them), may seem normal to us, but it's a new phenomenon in the course of human history.

My (Jeff's) son Brenton once shared a college writing assignment in which he explored how American films reflect changing attitudes toward poverty. His takeaway was striking: Over time, movies have shifted from portraying poverty as a communal challenge to framing it as an individual burden. While his sample was small and informal, I think he identified a meaningful cultural trend—from "we're in this together" to "you're on your own."

Consider the movie *It's a Wonderful Life*, where George Bailey sacrifices personal ambition to serve his community.[2] In a pivotal scene, he pleads with panicked townspeople during a bank run: "We've got to stick together." The film's resolution—neighbors rallying to save Bailey's business—underscores the power of collective support. The message is clear: Community is the safety net.

Contrast that with *Rocky*, where the titular character escapes poverty not through community but sheer personal grit.[3] Rocky's world is isolating, even hostile. His rise comes through solitary training and determination, culminating in the iconic montage of him summiting the steps of the Philadelphia Museum of Art alone. His triumph is framed not as a shared victory but as proof that individual effort can overcome all.

These films, decades apart, reflect a broader cultural shift—from interdependence to independence.

A Failed Experiment

Think for a moment about how our lives are designed—not by intention but because of convenience and affluence—for independence. We have emergency roadside assistance built into our auto insurance so that we can call for help any time it's needed. We'll never have to interrupt a friend's day with a plea for roadside rescue. Many of us park our cars in the garage at the end of the workday, entering our houses without even a chance encounter with a neighbor. Gone are the days of calling (or texting) a neighbor because we ran out of eggs while mixing a batch of cookie dough. It's not all that inconvenient to drive to the store or—better still—have an unknown, generously tipped shopper deliver eggs to our doorstep.

Our spiritual lives are also defaulting toward independence. According to Barna Group research, more than half of Christians in the United States (56 percent) believe our spiritual life is entirely private.[4] In a related research study, Barna found that even in the area of discipleship, traditionally pursued one-on-one or communally, fully 38 percent preferred an independent pursuit . . . to go it alone.[5]

When young adult church attendees were asked, "Why do you participate in your community of worship?" they were given the opportunity to select as many reasons as they found applicable, yet only 14 percent said they attend church because someone in their worship community cares deeply about them.[6] Survey participants neither expected nor experienced deeper relationships or community as an aspect of gathering with other followers of Jesus. In a world longing for connection, we've lost sight of a key distinctive of the church: deep, caring, interdependent relationships in which we live out Jesus' command to "love one another." Regrettably, we're operating as independently as any other group, relegating the church's role to one that is but a fraction of what God intended.

While bemoaning the decreasing relevance of the church in our society, Christ-followers in the United States seem to have forgotten, or redefined, the role the church is intended to play in our lives. Eric Costanzo, Daniel Yang, and Matthew Soerens, authors of the book *Inalienable: How Marginalized Kingdom Voices Can Help Save the American Church*, argue that our "exclusively individualistic approach to biblical interpretation and ecclesiology is a misunderstanding of what is the majority context of the Bible: people living in community." Even our English Bible translations tend to obscure the fact that most of the New Testament is written in "second-person plural, to 'y'all,' not just to 'you.'"[7] While we are called to a personal relationship with God, Scripture is clear: Our journey as Christ's followers is together. It's personal but not private. It is *we*, not *me*. Our faith was always intended to be lived out in community.

Still, we relate to the independent streak that runs through American discipleship. Raised in evangelical families, we were shaped by rich faith traditions modeled by our parents. While our churches did have communal practices, they strongly emphasized "personal quiet time" where we learned to seek God and read the Bible alone and think about how the day's passage spoke to us personally. There is a very real need for solitude, communing with God in prayer, reflection, and listening—all of which we practice in our lives today. However, Jesus does not call us to independently follow him on our own. He prayed for the unity of his followers, that we would love each other. We don't do that alone! Scripture was meant to be understood in the context of community, and we experience the richness and closeness of Jesus best when we experience it in community with others.

Jesus Prayed for Something Different

Operating interdependently, seemingly untroubled by making their independent mark on the world, our teachers in savings groups around the world have lifted a veil from our eyes, helping us glimpse a core part of the kingdom. The apostle Paul put it this way:

> For by the grace given me I say to every one of you: Do not think of yourself more highly than you ought, but rather think of yourself with sober judgment, in accordance with the faith God has distributed to each of you. For just as each of us has one body with many members, and these members do not all have the same function, so in Christ we, though many, form one body, and each member belongs to all the others. (Romans 12:3-5)

Each body part contributes greatly to the whole, but no single part was designed to pursue greatness apart from it. God created us to belong to and contribute to a body. It is precisely what Jesus prayed for in John 17 the night before he died. He prayed that we'd experience the essence of the kingdom, which reflected his nature: relationship.

> I'm praying not only for them but also for those who will believe in me because of them and their witness about me. The goal is for all of them to become one heart and mind— just as you, Father, are in me and I in you, so they might be one heart and mind with us. Then the world might believe that you, in fact, sent me. The same glory you gave me, I gave them, so they'll be as unified and together as we are—I

in them and you in me. Then they'll be mature in this oneness, and give the godless world evidence that you've sent me and loved them in the same way you've loved me. (John 17:20-23 MSG)

Jesus was praying for his disciples gathered with him that night. But he was also praying for *us*, as those who would go on to believe because of their witness. Jesus was compelling his disciples to do more than just be together. They had been *around* each other almost nonstop for about three years. He was painting a picture to inspire them to see there is even more: the experience of interdependence. Biblical scholar Tim Mackie shares a metaphor that helps us identify the difference.

Consider a bag of marbles and a cluster of grapes. A bag of marbles comprises many individual balls, each with a significant range of movement. Some marbles could fall out of the bag without affecting the others. Grapes are also individual entities, yet each grape in a cluster is connected to the same source of life. If a grape falls off the stem, it leaves a noticeable gap. Although no single grape touches all the others at once, each remains part of the same cluster—connected, interdependent, and affected by what happens to the whole. In the same way, we grow together as we remain communally connected to the vine (John 15:1-17). Mackie compares this to our Christian community: "The gospel creates a community of people who are personally being impacted, transformed, and brought into this organic thing that takes place when the story of Jesus is told. It's personal—but it is never private." Our faith is meant to play out in the context of an interdependent community. Sounds a lot like *koinōnia*.

There should be significant differences between a group of Christ-followers and an aggregation of individuals who share a common interest but aren't "there for each other and because of each other." Mackie concludes, "The great challenge of any Christian community is the constant temptation to drift from becoming what ought to be—which is a cluster of grapes—to becoming a bag of marbles."[8]

A few years ago, I (Phil) recognized that I spoke of savings groups as bags of marbles, bringing my own bent toward individualism and independence to the narrative. I'd talk about Roseline who built a house; Pierre who opened a business; or Beatrice who expanded her land ownership, planted more crops, and finally had enough produce to feed her children. All of these stories were worth celebrating, but as I sat with savings group members around the world, I realized these snapshots were viewed through my own lens of individual accomplishment. In reality, they neither communicated the full story nor mirrored the way group members themselves would tell it. Group members saw themselves as clusters of grapes.

While I focused on personal successes, savings group members told stories of transformation that would not and could not exist outside the context of community. Beatrice would share that she never felt capable of managing more land until her group members encouraged her. Pierre would recall that fellow savings group members took a chance on him, allowing him to borrow their pooled resources to launch that business—and trusting him to repay their life savings. Roseline would share how her group labored alongside her to make the bricks that built her home. And almost without exception, all would say, "Through this journey, my brothers and sisters loved, cared for, and encouraged me. I could not have done this without them. We are a family." Their perspective on the communal nature of flourishing gradually reshaped my own.

Interdependent Creations

In my (Jeff's) suburban Oklahoma City yard, there are ten oak trees likely older than I am. To me, they've always symbolized strength and independence. The expression, "Mighty oaks from little acorns grow" seems to speak to independent self-actualization. But as I've studied and contemplated how God's kingdom principles are visible in creation, I've learned that trees don't tell a story of independence. They are one of the best visual representations of how God has embedded his interdependent nature into creation.

Trees are linked to each other through an underground network of fungi that operates like the neural pathways in the human brain. Though they are separate plants, the trees are so integrated that, in many ways, they function as a single unit. In one study, a Douglas fir injured by insects seemed to signal a nearby pine tree via a chemical that traveled through the fungi to warn the neighboring tree about the insects' danger.[9] In response, the pine tree produced a chemical to ward off the insects and protect itself.

Still more surprising, trees share nutrients. Established trees might pass along carbon and other nutrients to a tree that's depleted. The trees also supply the fungi with nutrients they require to survive, just as the trees receive indispensable nutrients from the fungi network. For trees, "all flourishing is mutual," as plant ecologist Robin Kimmerer Wall has written.[10] One tree cannot flourish without the fungi network and proximate trees also thriving. *Independence and flourishing are opposed to each other.* That's true under the ground, where God has created even trees and fungi to flourish interdependently, and it's true above the ground as well—though we frequently operate in defiance of that truth.

Kelly Kapic artfully expands on this idea:

> God made us as *creatures*. And the *good* part about being a creature is we were made to be dependent upon God and, by our very design, also dependent on other people and the earth. . . . Dependence goes against a lot of our instincts. Just think about how we use the language of dependence in our culture. It's usually negative. It's one of the reasons we struggle with community. . . . Often what we're missing is the good of dependence. We need to cultivate an awareness of how our dependence and our needs open avenues of love.[11]

In chapter two, we described the *koinōnia* way of life as characterized by shared identity, shared purpose, and shared experience. These three characteristics also guide us as we seek to depend on each other the way God created and Jesus intended. We must understand our true identity—beings created in God's image, unconditionally loved by him, and called to reflect his nature—and build our understanding of purpose from that identity. With that shared purpose in mind, we must set about creating a life of interdependence by intentionally prioritizing shared experiences with others, ultimately leading to interwoven lives.

Shared Identity, Shared Purpose

For most of our adult lives, we've held to the idea that every person has a unique, God-given purpose to fulfill. Something that no one else can do, that, if discovered, would ensure a life of meaning and significance. It's been a dominant narrative in US Christian subculture, perhaps unsurprisingly, because a slightly less "Christianized" version of that same story is our society's dominant narrative.

But adding the words "God-given" does not stop this from being a *self*-focused pursuit. Our purpose isn't hidden or waiting to be discovered. God has, in fact, given all of us a purpose: We are made to share in his work of nurturing his creation. We do this by loving God and loving our neighbor. We are made to reflect God's character in our world and to care for the people and things around us. Understanding this shared purpose changes everything about how we relate to each other.

We can reflect God's nature in every area of our lives—like how we do our work and how we use our time, money, and influence—but the primary way we reflect God's nature is in relationships. Jesus showed us what it's like to truly be God's image as a human. He served and sought the best for others, not only for his friends but also for his enemies. Jesus summarized how to be a human in God's image in the Sermon on the Mount (Matthew 5–7): a master class on interdependent living.

Being there for each other is a part of our created purpose, but we're pushed in a different direction by the culture we're experiencing and co-creating with our fellow human beings. Deep in our spirits we retain that knowledge of original, unadulterated purpose, and this is precisely why people at the end of their lives don't express regret for the love and care they've placed into their relationships. Many, however, express regret for working to make an independent and unique mark on the world at the expense of relationships.[12] With the perspective of a lifetime, being there for each other always wins out.

Designing an Interdependent Life

In the fall of 2023, author and entrepreneur Liz Bohannon visited Life.Church to talk about loneliness. In a winsome way, she delivered hard-hitting truth, suggesting that the problem of aloneness isn't something someone else is imposing on us. "We are designing," she explained, "an entire culture with the primary values of convenience, of independence, of privacy, of comfort. And while none of those things are inherently wrong or bad . . . we are going to get certain results from that design."[13] The word that stuck with us is "design." We will get the life we design, so if we want something different, we must *design* our lives differently. Being part of a *koinōnia* community won't happen by accident.

In the last chapter, we pointed out that one aspect of the *koinōnia* way of living that Luke describes in Acts is shared experience. The "advantage" early followers of Jesus had was that they were persecuted and poor. Both conditions pushed them to live in proximity and dependence, with shared experiences and realities. Their survival depended on it. Something similar could be said of those we've met in savings groups in the world's underserved communities: To overcome their common enemy of poverty, they're going to have to band together. Even with the extra nudges toward community, these are *design* decisions.

Choosing to experience the interdependence to which Jesus calls us will, for most of us, require a redesign. Here are some suggestions on how we might design an interdependent life. We'll carry this theme of "designing a life" into the remaining "one-another" chapters.

Start with the heart. Interdependence begins with our heart posture. The apostle Paul instructed the Philippians,

> If you have any encouragement from being united with Christ, if any comfort from his love, if any common sharing in the Spirit, if any tenderness and compassion, then make my joy complete by being like-minded, having the same love, being one in spirit and of one mind. Do nothing out of selfish ambition or vain conceit. Rather, in humility value others above yourselves, not looking to your own interests but each of you to the interests of the others. (Philippians 2:1-4)

Henri Nouwen put it this way:

> Community is first of all a quality of the heart. It grows from the spiritual knowledge that we are alive not for ourselves but for one another. Community is the fruit of our capacity to make the interests of others more important than our own. . . . The question, therefore, is not "How can we make community?" but "How can we develop and nurture giving hearts?"[14]

Nouwen is right; *koinōnia* occurs when the condition of our hearts makes space for it and compels us to build a life with others in mind. Designing a life of interdependence begins in prayer, asking God to develop within us a heart inclined toward others and not toward our own interests.

Deepen connections with next-door neighbors. Christy and I (Jeff) have lived in several homes during our thirty-plus years of marriage. I'm embarrassed to admit that in some of these homes, I barely met our neighbors and certainly didn't build any kind of genuine relationships. We've lived in our current house for a decade, and we hope to be here for many years. A few years ago, we made a commitment to modify our habits to get to know our neighbors. We invite them over for dinner, and we take more walks through the neighborhood, stopping to chat as we go. These regular touchpoints have helped us better understand the highs and lows of their lives, and we're increasingly able to be there for each other. One of my good friends, Felix, passed away unexpectedly while I was writing this book. Felix and his wife embraced the simple habit of sitting with neighbors on their driveway several evenings a week instead of sitting on their back porch. What they gave up in privacy they recouped in conversation that led to connection and deeper friendships. After Felix passed away, a large group of neighbors gathered in a driveway in his honor to celebrate how he brought them together.

Create margin. To be there for one another, we need to be *available* when someone wants to talk or needs a helping hand. If our schedules are so full that we are always on the go, it's hard to be present when help is required, even if we have laid the relational groundwork. For most of us, designing a life of interdependence will involve doing less and being more present and available. Set aside a few minutes to browse through your calendar over the last one or two months. How much of your time was unscheduled? Have you designed a life with enough margin to be spontaneously available to others? Living interdependently requires us to do less to create more margin.

Call a friend. We're grateful for our culture's increased recognition of the importance of mental health and the vital role that professional counselors and therapists play. At the same time, we don't want to lose the impulse or ability to simply call a friend and share what's on our heart or ask for prayer support. These friendships can flourish where we've created margin and availability. So yes, find a licensed counselor. *And* call a friend.

Rethink our stuff. Designing a life of interdependence also involves rethinking our possessions. What if we viewed our things—particularly anything beyond basic essentials—as resources to share? Severe storms and tornadoes are a way of life where I (Jeff) live in Oklahoma's "Tornado Alley." Many newer homes include storm shelters where families can roll open a metal door to access a tiny underground room in the garage.

After living here for a decade and weathering many tornadoes, Christy and I recently invested in a storm shelter that's large enough to share with our neighbors. The day it was installed, we told each of them, "Our shelter is your shelter." We shared our garage code so they can access the shelter any time, even if we are not in town when a tornado warning is issued. It may not be a storm shelter, but we can all share little things more frequently. Instead of running to the store to grab an ingredient for a recipe, why not take the old-fashioned approach and see if the next-door neighbor has some to spare? And the next time you bake your favorite dessert, why not make some extra to share with that neighbor or a friend at work?

Depend on colleagues. Interdependence can also be integrated into our careers. Whatever the job, there are opportunities to influence others, directly or indirectly. For those in management or leadership, designing part of the work experience itself to build community among coworkers is a way to depend on each other. For example, managers can set the expectation that team members should seek one another's input and expertise.

Choosing to forgo some profits in exchange for paying employees a bit more for their work is another expression of God's generous heart and interdependent design. And all of us, whether we're in management or not, can lean on what others have to offer and be quick to acknowledge we can't do it alone. Set aside some time to seek advice from a coworker on how you can add even more value in your work.

Recognize the collective nature of discipleship. Regularly meeting with other followers of Jesus to pray and study the Bible together is foundational to interdependent living, as spiritual formation is where we most need each other. Whether meeting face-to-face or connecting digitally through the YouVersion Bible App or messaging groups, listen attentively to how God is shaping others and what you can learn from their experience. Others help realign our thoughts and actions with Jesus' kingdom way, so encourage each other, remind one another who we are in Christ, and challenge each other to relentlessly pursue Jesus' way of living.

There's No Going Back

Hannah and Kasie share a remarkably strong friendship. We assumed they'd followed the typical trajectory of favorable first impression to friendship until Hannah shared more of their story.

Hannah said she first noticed Kasie from a distance while serving at church. Because of Kasie's "always-put-together" exterior, Hannah concluded they would never be friends. A couple years later, their lives intersected in a far more personal way when Kasie was hired to fill a staff role Hannah was vacating. Although Hannah was excited about her new role on the same team, she couldn't help drawing comparisons and feeling replaced as she watched Kasie take on responsibilities that had once belonged to her.

Kasie was, admittedly, standoffish about becoming friends, having decided to keep firm boundaries between her professional and personal life. She was warm but guarded, friendly but distant. Over the following many months, what began as an awkward handoff morphed into unspoken tension.

For Hannah, transition was happening at home too. Newly married, she was praying for God to provide a close friend to walk with her in accountability as she adjusted to this new season of life. When Kasie shared in a team meeting that God was prompting her toward more gentleness in her relationships, Hannah felt God's nudge to ask Kasie to walk alongside her, though Kasie wasn't a natural choice.

Hannah hesitantly, obediently set a meeting, intent on becoming not just friends with Kasie but partners in spiritual growth. She began by expressing appreciation for Kasie's giftings and apologizing for the assumptions she'd held toward her colleague. Kasie reciprocated by confessing that her resolve to separate friendship and work had erected unnecessary walls. Then, Hannah shared the idea of becoming partners in spiritual growth, which would include a commitment to transparency and accountability, as well as praying for, challenging, and supporting each other. This level of relational interdependence was foreign to Kasie—and not altogether appealing—but she tentatively said yes, and they began meeting to talk once every two weeks.

This type of relationship was also new and strange to Hannah, though it had been her suggestion. "Most of the time, chemistry comes first, then friendship," Hannah pointed out. But Kasie and Hannah started with nothing more than a commitment to spend intentional time together, talking faithfully every two weeks. They didn't establish any agenda or framework for their conversations. They just committed to being together and trying to find ways to help each other grow as they conversed, integrating the core elements of *koinōnia* community: shared identity, shared purpose, and shared experience. About eighteen months into their relationship, they realized they had developed an intense bondedness, friendship, and love. "Best friends" doesn't even describe it.

"My relationship with Hannah has made everything better in my life," Kasie says. "Before I knew Hannah, I was happy with my life and marriage, but I didn't know what I was missing out on and how much I needed it. I'm never going back." Listening to Hannah and Kasie's story, we felt as if we were hearing someone explain what it might have been like to experience the *koinōnia* that Acts 2 describes among the earliest followers of Jesus.

We were especially moved by how Hannah and Kasie talked about their level of openness with each other. "We all need thought partners," Hannah said. "The kind of thing where we can say the thoughts we have in our head that we're embarrassed that we are even thinking. When I say the things in my thoughts out loud to Kasie, all of a sudden, the lies and insecurities that create anxiety lose their power, and they fade away." Kasie and Hannah experience life from fully depending on each other.

We asked Kasie how she'd respond to someone who still isn't convinced that giving up a life of independence is worth it.

Living life with others is hard. It introduces challenges and discomforts that you have to push through in order to build relationships and sustain community. And living life alone is hard. The research is undeniable: Choosing to not engage with community decreases life satisfaction, negatively impacts our physical health, and is contrary to the example Jesus set for us as he walked the earth. You have a choice in which hardship you want to live with: the one with temporary difficulty or the one that extends far beyond a temporary feeling.

I dare you to believe this could be worth it. The truth is, you won't likely realize the full power of interdependent living until you begin experiencing the fruit of your commitment. And let me tell you, the fruit will grow and ripen! But I dare you to believe in it. God's Word and Jesus' example were too clear for us to question it: Living a life surrounded by trusted friends will spur us on as we pursue living out Christ's will and will even make the journey more joyful!

Once we taste a life of interdependence, there's no going back.

Reflect Individually

- If someone made a movie about your life, what role would interdependence play in your story?

- How would living more interdependently change your life for the better? What would be the cost?

- In what ways do you lean on your church community for support? How does your church community depend on you for support?

- Looking back through the "Designing an Interdependent Life" section of this chapter, what ideas stand out to you as important? How will you act on those ideas?

Discuss Together

- Would you describe our group as a bag of marbles or a cluster of grapes? How could we live more like a cluster of grapes?

- In what ways do we depend on each other for spiritual formation?

- How well do we spend time together, cultivating shared purpose, identity, and experience?

- In what ways do you see yourself as part of the body, and in what ways do you see yourself as an individual?

4

KNOW ONE ANOTHER

There is no fear in love.
But perfect love drives out fear.

1 JOHN 4:18

LATE ONE SUNDAY AFTERNOON more than thirty years ago, I (Phil) found myself sitting in my car, buffeted by waves of discouragement, confusion, and depression. I was in my thirties, a family man with a wonderful wife and a four-year-old son, working in Houston's bustling business sector. I was successful in my career and known by friends, church acquaintances, and extended family as a good person and a model Christian. With the exception of the last few months, I'd been a lifelong church attendee and was generally considered a very responsible person—the kind who could be counted on.

All of that now seemed to be imploding. I felt the weight of my current reality: separated from my wife; living in a hovel of an apartment furnished with only a card table, a folding chair, and a mattress; having an affair that I had not only hidden from my wife but outright lied about; not allowed to spend unsupervised time

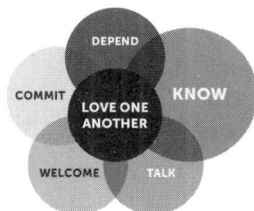

with my son because my intense and growing addiction to cocaine left me unpredictable and irresponsible. I felt a deep sense of shame as I painfully pondered what had gone wrong. How could I face members of my and Becca's extended families, close family friends, or fellow congregants at the church where I hadn't shown my face in over three months?

On this Sunday afternoon, my discouragement, confusion, and depression were accompanied by a last gasp of determination to escape my current reality. The cocaine binges were out of control. The drug-induced highs were followed by progressively deeper and darker lows that had begun to include not only thoughts but plans of taking my life. The tight grip of addiction, combined with the shame and destruction caused by my failures, seemed too great to live with. And I was alone with it all. Fearing for my life, I called an older couple I knew to be strong Christians. I asked if I could come by to talk. Knowing they had spare bedrooms in their "empty nest," I planned to ask if they would allow me to stay with them, providing a "safe house," a sanctuary from my current volatile environment.

As I'd shared with them the intense and humiliating details of my current reality, I'd sensed unease and even disdain in their faces and tone, if not their words outright. In desperation, I'd asked anyway—*Could I live with you?*—and the couple agreed: with one condition. "If you ever come into the house with cocaine or high on cocaine, or if we ever find you've been using, you're out. Understood? Agreed?" I agreed.

Now sitting in my car outside their house and reflecting on the meeting, my discouragement grew stronger. The tenor of the interaction had been more judgmental than supportive, more condemning than sympathetic. And the crescendo of the "one condition" felt oppressive and demeaning. Not that I could blame them, and not that I intended to fall off the wagon, but what if I did? I knew how volatile I was, how the addiction rendered me weak, breaking down my desperate desire to leave it behind. I longed for a truly safe place. While this space was physically safe, the couple had been clear there would be little tolerance or support. I wept as a familiar sense of doom began to overtake me again. And then, in what I believe was a Holy Spirit moment, I thought of Bill.

Two years earlier, Bill filled the pulpit one Sunday morning at church. He was a successful businessman and a church elder. His wife, Nancy, and their teenage children were also very involved in the congregation. Bill was a soft-spoken man, warm and engaging in conversation—one of those people who seemed comfortable in his own skin and somehow made others feel the same. His sermon that Sunday was somewhat unorthodox. He shared a long, parable-like story about a man who nearly lost it all—career, family, life—through excessive drinking, womanizing, and immoral business dealings. He shared some raw and ugly stuff I wasn't accustomed to hearing in church. The story then turned to God's reconciling love for the man. A story of desperate brokenness and undeserved grace. It wasn't your typical sermon, but it was powerful.

At the conclusion of his discourse, Bill dropped an "oh, by the way" that elicited an audible gasp from the congregation, myself included. "Oh, by the way," Bill said quietly and assuredly, "the man whose story I just shared? That man is me." Following the gasp, the congregation sat in stunned silence as Bill gathered his notes and sat down. I recall how my respect for Bill had only grown because he shared so vulnerably.

Bill and I weren't close friends; in fact, we'd never interacted beyond the occasional pre- or post-service chat. But in this

Spirit-ordained moment, and in my desperation, I found Bill's number, dialed the phone, and asked if I could stop by. That afternoon and well into the evening, I found my sanctuary. Bill and Nancy listened, cared, empathized, and even hugged me as I poured out my heart. There was no judgment and no conditions, for they, too, had traveled a similar path. They offered a spare bedroom and a place at their table for as long as I needed. They also offered listening ears, a sounding board, and loving encouragement over the weeks to come, as I tried to put my life back together. Even when I fell off the wagon a couple of times (and Bill and Nancy knew it), their love was unwavering. They met my brokenness with empathy and encouragement. "We're sorry. We understand; it doesn't feel good. We're with you. You can do this."

By God's grace, I was able to break my addiction to cocaine, and Becca and I slowly and painfully reconciled. I could write volumes about Becca's long-suffering and compassion through the entire process. I battled a lot of shame and felt beyond unworthy, yet over time, her *ezer*-like compassion was transformative in my journey to forgive and accept myself.

Bill and Nancy saved my life: Bill, in his willingness to be known, openly and vulnerably sharing the most difficult parts of his past. And both Bill and Nancy in providing a desperately needed safe place, where I, too, could be known and fully loved and accepted, even in my brokenness. God used their words and their actions for my redemption. Their vulnerability and unconditional acceptance were like a pebble dropped in a pool, creating divine ripples that God continues to work through even to this day.

Bill and Nancy have passed away. They've received a resounding "well done" from Jesus. They have no idea of those divine ripples— how God has used and continues to use their sacrificial act of being known. But I do. Deeply, I do.

A Paradox

Several years after my life-changing encounter with Bill and Nancy, now living in the Northeast, I was asked to consider joining the senior leadership board of the church our family then attended. The process included a series of conversations and interviews with current church leaders, allowing them to get to know me at a deeper level. I could not honestly answer their questions without revealing my past—yet the prospect of confessing a history of drug addiction, suicidal ideation, and infidelity to those who were considering my fitness for church leadership terrified me.

The thought of full disclosure filled me with dread, even in the small, confidential circle in which I'd be sharing. It wasn't just the prospect of being rejected as a leader. Confidentiality doesn't always hold. People talk, word could get out, and my story would be a great morsel to feed the church gossip chain. "Don't tell anyone, but confidentially, I heard that Phil . . . We should pray for him." The risk of tarnishing my well-crafted and guarded persona, of no longer being accepted, loomed ominously. My dread grew so strong that I considered politely declining the invitation altogether. Could the value of being known possibly outweigh the potential cost of being exposed?

It is truly a paradox. Although we are hardwired for and crave relationships in which we are fully known and fully loved, we are also risk-averse and pain-avoidant people. We want to be loved but also safe, and these longings live in tension. The paradox creates a cycle of longing, shame and hiding. We fear that the better someone knows us—a precondition for the meaningful relationships we crave—the less likely they will be to accept us. Our fear of losing the connection we have leads us to hide the parts of ourselves we consider unworthy, effectively blocking deeper connection.

I long for meaningful relationships where I'm known and loved.

Longing

Hidden   **Shame**

It is better to hide the parts I don't like than to risk not being accepted.

I fear that if others knew me like I know me, I would not be worthy of their friendship.

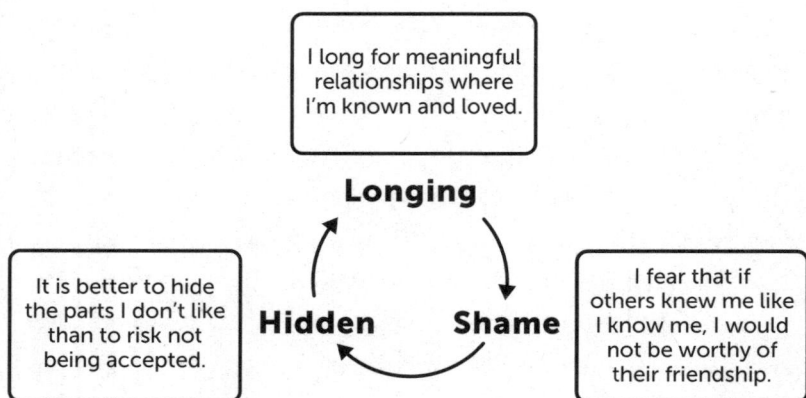

Research professor and author Brené Brown devoted years to researching the human desire for connection. After assessing thousands of interviews, she concluded that what stood in the way of relational connectedness was captured in one word: *shame*.[1] The more we experience shame—the personal, internalized belief that we are not good enough, falling short, and therefore not acceptable—the less able we are to practice vulnerability. Shame leads to an internal narrative that says, "If they *really* knew me, I would not be deserving of connection."

Brown's groundbreaking research takes us right back to the Garden of Eden, where Adam and Eve, in full knowledge of their sinfulness, fruitlessly sewed fig leaves and forsook connection with their Creator. They took on the internal narrative: *shame*. And the natural response to shame is to hide those parts of ourselves that we believe are just not good enough to be seen and accepted. As John Lynch, coauthor of *TrueFaced*, describes being hidden, Adam began it, but through the ripples of centuries, you and I have turned hiding into an art form.[2]

The result? More than half of people surveyed (54 percent) say they sometimes or always feel as though no one knows them well.[3] With roughly 13 percent of American adults living alone,[4] the data suggests that many who are not physically isolated are leading emotionally isolated lives.

Feeling Not Good Enough

It doesn't take a major misstep or moral failure to trigger shame. In fact, most of the shame we carry is not from a past or present sin but from the things we see as flaws, failures, or areas in which we believe we don't measure up.

In an insightful article for *Christianity Today*, author Hannah Anderson illustrates how our shame blocks connection. Anderson's husband worked as a pastor of a small church. Despite their frugal lifestyle, his $28,000 salary couldn't cover their expenses when they became a family of five, with Anderson fully occupied raising three children under the age of five and volunteering at the church. They easily qualified for food stamps—a helpful and necessary benefit— but Anderson couldn't stop wondering how others might perceive their use of supplemental nutrition benefits, a form of welfare.

"Shame . . . grew each time I ran into a congregant or neighbor at the store. . . . I felt they would judge me if they knew how I kept my family fed." Too many times she had heard callous assumptions that welfare recipients were lazy or milking the system. "I knew we weren't idle. . . . But because of the messages I'd heard, I also couldn't shake the sense that I was doing something wrong. And if I was in the wrong, I felt I had to hide what I was doing."

She recalls standing in the grocery store checkout line one day when Rhonda, the church organist, queued up behind her.

> Normally, I would ask about her grandbabies or garden, but instead, I mumble an excuse about having forgotten bread and navigate my cart out of line toward the aisles stocked with food. But I haven't forgotten anything. It's a charade, a charade

brought about by the shame I feel because my family is on welfare, and Rhonda is about to see me pay with food stamps.

Because of shame, Anderson writes, "I felt isolated from and abandoned by the very people I worshipped beside every Sunday."[5]

Sometimes our shame seems *most* pronounced among fellow believers, contributing to a sense of isolation in our churches. Nearly half of adults ages eighteen to thirty-five (49 percent globally, 47 percent of Christians, and 67 percent of church dropouts) conclude, "People at church are judgmental."[6] Almost a century ago, German theologian Dietrich Bonhoeffer wrote of the behavior-based expectations Christians place on ourselves and one another. Although he references sin, his words apply equally to any other source of shame.

> It may be that Christians, notwithstanding corporate worship, common prayer, and all their fellowship in service, may still be left to their loneliness. The final break-through to fellowship does not occur, because, though they have fellowship with one another as believers and as devout people, they do not have fellowship as the undevout, as sinners. The pious fellowship permits no one to be a sinner. So everybody must conceal his sin from himself and from the fellowship. We dare not be sinners. Many Christians are unthinkably horrified when a real sinner is suddenly discovered among the righteous. So we remain alone with our sin, living in lies and hypocrisy. The fact is that we are sinners![7]

We could rephrase, "We have fellowship as the redeemed but not as the ashamed. The fact is, we are all ashamed of something!"

The propensity to pretend that because we have Jesus we have overcome every sin or struggle and are living victorious, beatific lives makes church one of the places where we are most prone to hide. In fact, 83 percent of pastors say they know someone who distanced themselves from the church as a result of a personal crisis. The most common reason given was, "I felt I couldn't be honest about myself and my life."[8] What's a Christian to do when the joy of the Lord doesn't seem to be giving us strength and we feel like less than conquerors? Might we be the weakest link among the fellowship of believers?

Bankrupt

Fifteen years ago, I (Jeff) was fearing judgment as I anxiously drove to Kincaid's, a local hamburger joint in Fort Worth, Texas, for a final interview for my first role with Life.Church. The previous weekend, I had endured a whirlwind of rigorous interviews. This lunch over some superbly greasy hamburgers was to be a less formal conversation to finalize the process.

But I was not sure the process would be finalized; even the prospect of the conversation I was about to have embarrassed me. While driving, I rehearsed how I planned to disclose my current life situation. I was convinced that what I needed to share might be a deal-breaker for a church.

In 1999, I founded Nexlead, an organization focused on helping schools, universities, and churches develop emerging young leaders using interactive content and immersive learning experiences. I led Nexlead through many years of growth. Then, in 2007, the organization financially imploded. In retrospect, I could see how my poor leadership and lack of forethought contributed to its demise.

This failure humiliated me in many ways. It pervaded not only my work life but also my home, as my family incurred the organization's financial obligations. I had no way to repay these debts. I was bankrupt, and this highly public failure shook the deepest part of my identity.

I was unsure if a church would be willing to hire someone who was, at the moment, spending time in bankruptcy court. I vividly remember sharing the details of my bankruptcy with the team of interviewers as we sat across from one another and ate our hamburgers—and I'll never forget my relief at their response. They did not flinch. In fact, they each went on to share the details of their own broken stories. They didn't have to, but they met my vulnerability with theirs. These first steps toward knowing and accepting one another changed the course of my life.

Worthy

Truth be told, I didn't want to go first in being known, but when I did, I experienced greater acceptance than I could have anticipated. I imagined my disclosure would block connection, but instead, it created connection, opening the door for others to share their struggles. They weren't facing bankruptcy, so the particulars were different, but it was as though I said, "I'm struggling"—and they all said, "Me too."

I (Phil) became known at a point of utter desperation. I first experienced the sting of rejection from those who, although they were believers, were seemingly not able to see their own brokenness reflected in mine or to respond reciprocally. But in Bill and Nancy, I experienced the salve of being seen, known, and loved anyway. I experienced the power of *ezer* and *allēlōn* put in practice.

If being known is so healing but shame is so universal, is there any hope of overcoming our impulse to hide? How can we step out of the cycle of shame and know one another without the pressure of our lives or vocations on the line? Brené Brown distilled a single variable that separates those who embrace being known from those who remain hidden: *worthiness*. According to Brown, "The people who have a strong sense of love and belonging believe they are worthy of love and belonging."[9]

Brown's conclusion reminded me (Phil) of a three-day silent retreat Becca and I once attended at a Catholic retreat center. One of my primary takeaways was the practice of sitting, hands opened upward, and reciting simple truths. The first of those truths was simply this: "God loves me, and I love myself." We were taught to say it quietly, let the words sink in; say it again, let it sink in; say it again, let it sink in. I've carried this simple practice with me for years.

"God loves me, and I love myself" is the counternarrative to the shame that urges us to remain hidden.[10] God (who sees and knows all) loves me. I can love myself. I am worthy. Not he loves me *if* or he loves me *when*, but he loves my whole, broken self. Full stop.

No amount of humanistic self-love will free us from the shackles of shame. But God's love—and his message of our unconditional worthiness—is powerful. While followers of Christ are certainly not immune from feeling shame or insufficiency, we should be first to embrace the vulnerability of being known, because through Christ's unconditional love, the unworthy are made worthy.

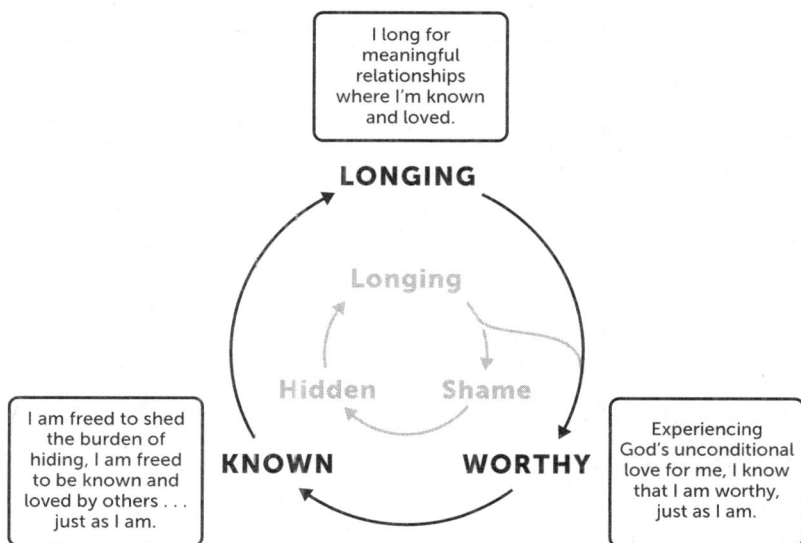

I long for meaningful relationships where I'm known and loved.

LONGING

Longing

Hidden　　Shame

KNOWN　　　　**WORTHY**

I am freed to shed the burden of hiding, I am freed to be known and loved by others . . . just as I am.

Experiencing God's unconditional love for me, I know that I am worthy, just as I am.

Jesus said the two greatest commandments are "Love the Lord your God" and "love your neighbor *as yourself*" (Mark 12:30-31, emphasis added). Volumes have been written on these words, but one observation is particularly relevant: When we understand that we are fully seen, known, and loved by Christ, we begin to extend that love to ourselves and others. Loving others—ultimately living a life marked by *ezer* (one to another), *allēlōn* (to each other), and *koinōnia* (each to all)—flows out of our heart and soul understanding and response to God's love for us, right now, just as we are.

Seen

While those who find themselves on the wrong side of biblical mandates and Christian cultural expectations tend to avoid our churches today, they were drawn to Jesus in his day. In fact, all types of people were drawn to him: rich and poor, Jew and Samaritan, religious and pagan, male and female, but particularly those who were on the fringe or marginalized.

Consider the Samaritan woman at Jacob's well (John 4). We know the conversation that took place, or at least the portion that was captured in Scripture. It was an amazing exchange on many levels. But the deeper dynamics of this encounter have often left us wondering.

The Samaritan woman came with her guard up. To Jesus' request, "Go, call your husband and come back," she replied, likely without missing a beat, "I have no husband." It was a well-rehearsed, probably well-used, factually true—but hidden—response. We can surmise that Jesus' request likely triggered an internal twinge of shame and fear of rejection—and with acceptance at stake, she knew what to omit from her story.

In response, Jesus let her know that she was seen and known. "You are right when you say you have no husband. The fact is, you have had five husbands, and the man you now have is not your husband. What you have just said is quite true." Jesus gave voice to the messy, painful truth she had tried to avoid. We've often pondered the "logical" reactions of shame, anger, despair, or even resentment that could have accompanied this uninvited disclosure. The woman might have thought, "How dare you?" or "What gives you the right?" or "You have no idea what my life has been like!" or "I feel bad enough; I don't need your pious judgment added to it!" Yet that wasn't her response. Why didn't she feel exposed?

There is a mystery the story doesn't explicitly reveal that is intimated in the woman's response. There's no sign of shame, anger, or resentment. Instead, she runs back to her village and with great excitement tells her neighbors they have to meet this man "who told me everything about myself."

It would seem that the page doesn't fully capture the very real and compelling love and acceptance that Jesus demonstrated to this woman. His words were factual. But rather than pious or condemning, his persona and tone must have been loving and accepting for the woman to leave the conversation not groping for a place to hide but celebrating being seen. Through Christ himself, she experienced God's design for each one of us to be fully known and fully loved.

Journey to the Other Side of Hidden

In some ways, savings groups, or even groups like Alcoholics Anonymous, have a head start when it comes to knowing one another. There's no pretense or pretending that everything is as it should be; membership is based on a mutual confession of need for one another. But it still requires a paradigm shift. Truly knowing each other cannot be mandated, and there are no shortcuts; it takes time.

Pascasie is a single mother in a rural community in Rwanda. For years after having a baby out of wedlock, Pascasie's former church friends called her *ikizira* (abomination). Most neighbors avoided her, and those who came to call generally brought complaints: about the stench emanating from her property because she lacked a pit latrine or about the behavior of her children, who weren't occupied by school—though they would have been if Pascasie could have afforded their school fees. "I was lonely, I was desperate. My kids were hungry," she recalls.

Pascasie was naturally guarded when Gilbert, a savings group promoter from another church denomination, came to visit, inviting her to join a savings group. Pascasie remembers his words: "Jesus loves you and he is for all." He went on to explain that this interdependent group, called *Ubumwe* (Unity), wasn't just willing to tolerate Pascasie's presence—they needed her. Pascasie soon joined the group in saving ten cents a week, but she wasn't yet ready to be known by the group.

Over time, as she heard others share openly about their lives, challenges, and emotions, she found that her difficulties were not unlike those of the other women in the group. She realized that she was not alone in her struggles or her longing to belong, and she began to see that this was a safe place to be known. "To me, *Ubumwe* group is not just a savings group; it is my second family. It is a place where I feel at home. It is a good place where I speak out my mind and cry when I want to cry."

The group's guiding Scripture is 2 Corinthians 5:17-19 (emphasis added):

Therefore, if anyone is in Christ, the new creation has come: The old has gone, the new is here! All this is from God, who reconciled us to himself through Christ and gave us the ministry of reconciliation: that God was reconciling the world to himself in Christ, not counting people's sins against them. And *he has committed to us the message of reconciliation.*

Ubumwe sought out the lonely (acting as *ezers*), they loved one another (*allēlōn*), and they did it in community (*koinōnia*).

As the savings group regularly reminds themselves, God reconciled us to him and gave us the ministry of reconciliation. Could it be that God intends for us to experience his love for us through others? We don't replace him with others, but we can experience his love for us and affirmation of our worthiness through others. Rather than compartmentalizing our relationships with God and others, could it be that they are inseparably intertwined? Our relationship with others is not an add-on but the embodiment of his kingdom.

Fellowship of the Broken

I (Phil) was still learning these lessons as I weighed the value of being known versus the potential fallout of being exposed by the members of the church board I had been invited to join. Sensing a nudge from God, I took the risk to be known.

In sharing openly during this interview, even before gauging the group's response to what I'd disclosed, I experienced an immediate internal release of tension, which was replaced by a sense of peace and joy. It was actually exhilarating—like removing a heavy backpack I'd been carrying for years. The hiding was behind me. I no longer needed to expend energy pretending to be a less-flawed version of myself. To my surprise, others in the group acknowledged that they, too, had walked through similar situations. Just as Jeff experienced with his Life.Church colleagues, I was welcomed into a fellowship of the broken.

The act of sharing with this group—"This is who I am, and I want you to know"—was the crescendo to experiencing God's love and hearing, as if from the Father himself, "You're okay; you're loved; you're worthy of belonging—just as you are." It came with a soul-level confirmation that it is good to be known.

It's easy to feel as though we are alone, the only ones facing issues, challenges, and past mistakes—at least mistakes of this magnitude. These fears keep us hidden. But here's the reality: a lot of folks are hiding big and small things from their past and even their present. We almost certainly know them—but because of hiddenness, we may not know that we know them.

Even when my crisis-driven confession of need was not well received by the couple I first approached in Houston many years prior, I still experienced God's transformative power in admitting that, despite what I had led my church family to believe, I was not okay. In my experience, these moments of being known are sacred. It is as though we are standing on holy ground, where we can experience God's transformative love.

Vulnerability Fosters Vulnerability

For us, Pascasie, and many others we talked with, allowing ourselves to be known opened the door to deeper relationships. Through vulnerability, we stepped into the "other side of hiddenness," a place where the greater connection we long for is waiting. Something else—something truly redemptive—can unexpectedly take place as we take that step. Our own vulnerability can open the door for others who are also longing to be known to take those same steps. Vulnerability fosters vulnerability.

Making ourselves known made us approachable to those who remained hidden. Many who are hidden long for a person with whom they can share openly, and when we allowed ourselves to be known, we became that safe place.

We are blessed to be part of churches that have intentionally, counterculturally chosen to navigate the rewarding, sometimes turbulent currents of being known. Our pastors and leaders do not feign perfection, and their willingness to be known as less-than-perfect humans has paved the way for congregants to follow suit, providing a space where people feel safe, regardless of shortcomings or struggles.

Over the years, both in small groups and church gatherings, we've heard brothers and sisters share amazing stories of their faith journeys, some displaying incredible vulnerability as together we push against Bonhoeffer's description of "pious fellowship." A married man shared his battle with addictions, a bubbly younger woman her struggles with depression, a middle-aged man his persistent doubt, and a husband and father the pain of his divorce. As members of these fellowships, we don't revel in the shortcomings, pain, or struggles. We revel in knowing each other and, in knowing, being able to better care for one another. We revel in knowing that we are seen, known, and loved in these safe, grace-filled families.

In the mutuality of *allēlōn* (to each other) and the power of *koinōnia* (each to all), the once hidden are used by God as healers, supporters, and encouragers to those who are yearning for a safe place. The forty-seven *allēlōn* (one another) commands in Scripture—for example, carry each other's burdens (Galatians 6:2), encourage one another (Hebrews 10:25), build each other up (Romans 14:19), and pray for each other (James 5:16)—presuppose our willingness to be known. Without knowing one another, it is impossible to fulfill these commands. We can't bear burdens, offer specific encouragement, or pray for others' personal needs when we do not know them. God invites us to be known and, in doing so, to help inspire others to be known.

Designing a Life of Knowing One Another

Hiding is our default response to shame. We noted earlier that we've turned it into an art form, but there's also an art to being known. We can make intentional design choices to push back against our propensity to hide.

Acknowledge our hiddenness. There are degrees of hiddenness, just as there are degrees of aloneness. No one can say, "I'm 100 percent known. No hiding here." So, the question is, what might I be hiding? Some questions to contemplate include: In what ways do I feel not good enough? What social pressures cause me to mask up? What motivates me to hide (how do I want to be perceived)? What's behind this? What's the risk of allowing myself to be known?

Seek out conversations. Perhaps you already have a friend you'd like to get to know on a deeper level or you can think of someone who is gracious, open, and willing to be known. (If this isn't the case, think of someone you would like to get to know, perhaps a work colleague, an acquaintance at church, or someone who shares common interests.) Take the first step by inviting them to spend time together in a setting that's conducive to conversation. Remember that relationships take time to grow, so don't expect "full disclosure" initially. Keep in mind that not every relationship will be "the right fit"—but time spent connecting with others is not wasted.

Consider affinity groups marked by openness and transparency. Some groups serve the specific purpose of establishing deeper connections and providing a safe place for sharing. Others, like the savings groups, may exist for a different primary purpose but find as they meet and get to know each other that the greater gift is the emergence of a loving *koinōnia* community where *allēlōn* relationships blossom. In both cases, groups that value and protect openness and transparency—living out biblical practices of *allēlōn*—are critical to the journey.

Choose what, when, and with whom to share. We intentionally incorporated examples in this chapter of one-on-one relationships, as well as individuals who shared vulnerably with a larger group. Sharing with a larger audience, as Bill did, may be a step for down the road or not at all, but most of us are looking for a safe and trusted person or a safe and trusted small group. Deciding what, when, and with whom to share are important, prayerful considerations.

What if it doesn't go well? What if our sharing unexpectedly opens doors of rejection, misunderstanding, or gossip? We are well aware of the risks. Because we are a community of imperfect followers of Jesus, our relationships are also imperfect. A dear friend of Becca's and mine (Phil's) suffered through a two-year bout with emotionally and physically debilitating depression. It was easily the darkest period of her life. In the process, she became the subject of the church's gossip chain when a group of friends violated her vulnerability. She has emerged stronger, wiser, and more grace-filled as a result, with sensitivity to others who've suffered similarly. But there's no denying the pain this gossip caused in an already painful season. She had to tighten her circle of transparency as a result, and we admire the way she did so with grace and discernment, devoid of bitterness or resentment.

Even for those who have been wounded, our encouragement is to not give up on being known. Once again, begin in prayer, asking God to help you trade resentment, bitterness, and pain for forgiveness and grace. As noted above, choosing what, when, and with whom you'll share is the next step. Pray for God to reveal ambassadors of "sanctuary." They are there. Finally, we have benefited from pastoral and professional counseling and would encourage this additional step to address deep wounds that have been inflicted.

Helping Others Move from Hidden to Known

Our willingness to be known encourages the same in others. If someone trusts you to truly know them, this is a sacred trust. Honor it in your response.

Listen . . . just listen. Many people need a safe place to talk or process. The art of actively listening, not to solve a problem but to seek to understand the heart of the sharer, is vital. Sometimes the only response that's needed will be connection: "I'm grateful that you've shared. I'm here." No quick-fix advice, no trying to provide the solution. Just being there, letting a person know they are loved and accepted, even if that time is spent in silence because it's too hard to talk. That's okay. They have no need to play a role, fake a smile, or hide their pain. A friend who is willing to just be there, just listen, is an immeasurable gift.

No judgment. The fears that prompt people to remain hidden are based in shame: for perceived failure, weakness, or insufficiency. Jesus' example should guide our response. He was regularly in the company of "sinners" and those who didn't measure up to society's standards. His message wasn't condemnation (that was reserved for the pious, religious elite!) but engagement and acceptance. We need a constant reminder: We are *all* sinners!

In the story of the woman caught in adultery (John 8), Jesus pushed back against those who saw the woman's sin and responded with judgment rather than love and grace. He forced them to see their own sin reflected in hers: "Let any one of you who is without sin be the first to throw a stone at her." The woman's accusers brought her before a crowd, but Jesus spoke with her one-on-one. He saw the sin but responded in love, wanting God's best for her and so inviting her, "Go now and leave your life of sin."

An important clarification on judgment: There is a difference between judgment and accountability. Accountability comes by invitation, with both parties' mutual desire to be supported, encouraged, and discipled toward a thriving life in Christ. Judgment, on the other hand, is generally unwelcome, unrequested, and—if we're honest with ourselves—can be rooted in our own critical spirit.

Hannah Anderson's experience using supplemental nutrition assistance brings up another important point. Those around her had *unknowingly* passed judgment on her. In their casual commentary on welfare recipients, they were dealing in judgment rather than compassion and grace. They never directed their comments at Anderson—and likely would not have, even if they knew she was accessing benefits—but she knew their beliefs from casual comments and callous conversation. Our suggestion would be to ask ourselves these questions: Are my comments and conversation rooted in a critical, judgmental spirit or filled with grace and compassion toward others? How might my words be causing others to remain hidden? "Hidden" people are watching and listening, discerning whether or not you, or even followers of Christ more broadly, are a safe space.

Acknowledge holy ground. Too often, we overlook the sacredness in someone's act of sharing. We should receive and care for what has been shared and the person who has shared it as treasures of immeasurable value. With very rare exceptions for safety, this sacred territory is also confidential territory. It is the sharer's prerogative to share with others; ours is to hold what has been shared as precious, honoring the risk that was taken in confiding in us.

Create "communities of the known." Being in a community of believers who practice mutual transparency is a treasured gift. But these communities are few and far between. Be the catalyst, both by leading the way in openness and transparency and by taking on the posture of an ambassador of relational safety. You may have to start with one or two friends, or perhaps you belong to a small group that's open to becoming that safe space. As you take these initial steps, you will find that you are not alone. People all around us are longing for a safe space to be themselves.

Reflect Individually

- What have you kept hidden, for fear of not being accepted?
- How might the benefits of being known outweigh the potential cost of being exposed?
- Who is a safe person or community that you can share with openly?
- How might you "go first" in vulnerability to open the door for others to go deeper?
- Pascasie was willing to be known after observing others' openness and vulnerability. Think of a time when you came out of hiding. What prompted you to do so? How did it make you feel? How was your openness received by others?

Discuss Together

- In what ways can this community (or small group) foster more open conversations?
- In what ways is our group a safe place? In what ways have we been less safe? What steps can we take to create a safer place to be known?
- Consider Bonhoeffer's statement about "the pious fellowship." How would our group look different if we were more honest about the ways we're still sinners or have otherwise fallen short?

5

TALK WITH ONE ANOTHER

Let us consider how we may spur one another on toward love and good deeds, not giving up meeting together, as some are in the habit of doing, but encouraging one another—and all the more as you see the Day approaching.

HEBREWS 10:24-25

THE FIRST TIME SPORTSWRITER Jonathan Tjarks attended a small group, he was nervous. "I remember walking up to the door and not knowing what to expect on the other side," he recalled. The threat lurking on the other side of his pastor's front door was a dozen people, all unknown to Tjarks, already engaged in conversation. "I didn't know what to do, so I did what most people would do: I headed over to the table with snacks."

Soon things kicked off with an icebreaker, and Tjarks remembered thinking, "Either I'm supposed to say I'm an alcoholic or this is a cult." But the plot took no interesting twists. It was, as advertised, a group where people sang, talked about the Bible, and prayed together. Sometime after "Amen," the pastor asked Tjarks if he'd come back, and he wasn't sure he would—but he did.

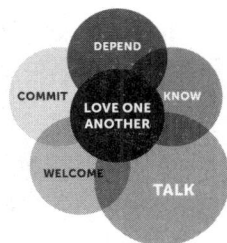

Over the next few years, the strangers gathered in that house became some of his closest friends. Tjarks doesn't claim it was always a delightful journey of discovery. "The people aren't always easy to deal with. You may not have a lot in common. You have to search for things to talk about. You can be vulnerable with people and they don't always respond how you would expect. And you certainly won't always agree with them on how they see the world." But through the steady investment of time and conversation, relationships deepened. "I was seeing the same people every week and I was telling them about my problems and they were telling me about theirs. Do that for long enough and you become friends. You get to know enough people that way and life group goes from being an obligation to something you look forward to."[1]

Through conversation, we enter into one another's lives. Rough edges are smoothed, assumptions questioned, and empathy gained. Through conversation, we come to see one another not simply for the ideologies we embrace but for the perspectives and experiences that led us there. "Conversation is the most human and humanizing thing that we do," wrote Sherry Turkle in a *New York Times* op-ed.[2] And we aren't doing enough of it.

We're hanging out and talking with each other less and less all the time. The American Time Use Survey is a government survey conducted each year by the Census Bureau that asks Americans how they spend their days. The survey started in 2003, and for the first decade, it consistently found that people spent about fifteen hours per week with their friends, including neighbors, coworkers outside work, and immediate and extended family. Then in 2014, the number of hours spent with others began to decrease and hasn't stopped declining. Since then, time spent with friends and family has dropped by nearly 50 percent, as time alone increased.[3] (Covid-19 certainly had an impact. Thankfully, 2023 data showed a slight correction. However, the negative trendline was well established before the pandemic and has persisted beyond it.)[4]

Increase in Time Spent Alone

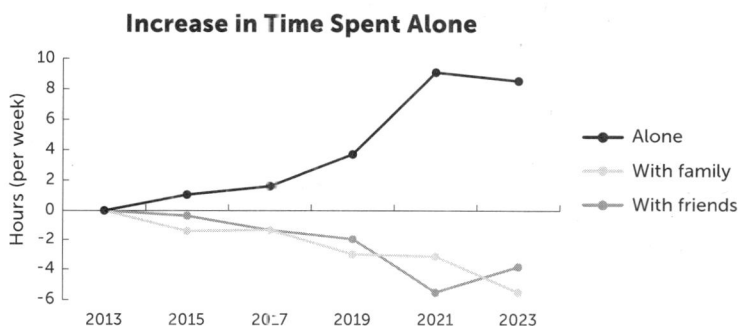

Even architecture reflects our growing alone time. Nolan Gray notes in *The Atlantic* that, for the most part, dining rooms are seen as an expendable feature in new apartment construction, "designing loneliness into American floor plans." More space is allocated to bedrooms and walk-in closets and less to shared space to eat. "As households and dining spaces have contracted, the number of people eating alone has grown. According to a 2015 report by the Food Marketing Institute, 'Nearly half the time we spend eating is spent in isolation, a central factor in America's loneliness epidemic and a correlate to a range of physical- and mental-health problems.'"[5]

Further, much of the time we do spend together can be termed "alone-together" time, when proximity doesn't translate to interaction: like a group gathered around a table engaging with their phones rather than one another. It's worth noting that smartphone ownership surpassed 50 percent in 2013, a milestone that likely contributed to the growing trend of spending time alone.[6] On average we check our phones almost once every five minutes we're awake, and in 2024 Americans spent an average of five hours every day with their eyes on a mobile phone screen.[7]

We've traded time with our friends and family for time shopping, dining, and exercising alone—but mostly for time with our screens.[8]

In addition to smartphones, streaming services have swelled our screentime. We now watch an average of over four hours per day of live television or streaming videos. That's a total of sixty full days each year![9] We can't help but conclude that this trend toward time spent alone—much of it consuming rather than creating—is a core contributor to the aloneness problem that exploded during the same period.

We, too, own smartphones and watch television. We'll confess that sometimes this mindless decompression is all we want to do at the end of a long day when our batteries are drained. But we have to be aware of the cost. There will always be a gravitational pull toward these low-energy pursuits, but the output matches the input: little investment, little reward.

Jonathan Tjarks admitted that often he didn't feel like going to small group. Sometimes he was tired or even tired of his fellow group members. But at the time of writing, he reflected, "I can't imagine not being in a life group at this point. Human beings aren't supposed to go through life as faces in a crowd." And without the good of conversation, we will never be anything more.

A Revolution in "Humanware"

In their book *The Talking Revolution*, authors Peter Osborn and Eddy Canfor-Dumas issue a challenge: "We've had a revolution in the technology that connects us around the world, in the hardware and the software—now we need a revolution in the 'humanware,' the *quality* of how we actually communicate with each other, one to one."[10]

The technological revolution that has brought so much life to our screens and offered us deeply engaging experiences has also pushed us to spend more time alone. To offset that growing trend, we must match that technological revolution with improvements in the quality of our communication. What if we were to trade some time alone for more time in conversation with our friends, neighbors, and family? What if we improved how we converse to make the most of our moments with others?

A conversation doesn't have to be heavy; it can be about our love for our favorite sports team, a recent vacation, or events from our day. Tjarks shared how conversation with others in his small group led to connection. There was probably a lot of sports talk, "How was your day?" chatter, and funny stories. But in Tjarks's words, it led to him sharing his problems with the others in the group, and they with him.

While this kind of connection might seem more natural for extroverts who are energized through interaction, humans of every variety long for connection. Introverts likely won't enjoy endless small talk, but good conversational skills help us and others move past superficial chattiness to talk about things that matter, including those topics we'd just as soon keep to ourselves: our hopes, fears, dreams, and heaviest burdens.

The kind of connection Tjarks experienced in his small group happens when we make our conversational partner the center of the conversation. It's one thing to be together, but it's another to pay attention to each other while together. Researchers found that even the presence of a phone on a table or within participants' peripheral vision changed both what was talked about and the degree of connection people experienced. "Even a silent phone disconnects us."[11]

Rather than stealing glances at our phones, we can engage in meaningful conversation and communicate our investment when we notice, ponder, and ask questions. Good conversation demands our full attention and our recognition that how and why we listen matters far more than what we say. We listen to understand others' interests, perspectives, passions, and problems, not to plan our next interjection or rehearse a story we're hoping to tell. We let curiosity lead and resist the urge to make our interests the center of the conversation. Excelling in conversation may not come naturally—it hasn't to either of us—but it can be learned.

Listen to Illuminate

Dr. Jackie Perry, creator of The Attuned Listener courses, has devoted her life to equipping people to be "empathic listeners." "As statistics on loneliness and mental health issues continue to rise," she explains, "equipping ordinary people to listen and lovingly hold space for a person's story has never been more important." She explains that while active listening is an excellent step in the right direction, curiosity helps us extend our connection even further because it invites us to explore people's complexity and the multiple elements or threads woven into and throughout their story.[12]

Approaching conversations with a listen-first approach requires incredible self-restraint. It is contrary to our norms in an independent society. It's not natural for most of us to set aside our need to tell someone about ourselves or share our expertise and instead be curious about what the world looks like from their perspective. Perry's conclusions reminded me (Jeff) of my earliest lessons in listening when I began my career.

I felt a mix of gratitude and pride when a church offered me a job right out of college: gratitude that they wanted me to join their staff and pride that they'd probably hired me because I had things pretty well figured out. Except that after I started, it seemed like very few people in the church or even on the staff were buying into my grand ideas.

One evening about six months after starting this new job, I was browsing a bookstore in the mall and stumbled on the leadership section. My previous experience with books was limited to novels, textbooks, or literature introduced to me in high school or college, so leadership books were an entirely new discovery.

I browsed the books and pulled one title off the shelf: *Principle-Centered Leadership* by Stephen R. Covey. I read the first few paragraphs and was captured by the words on the page. The issues the book raised spoke directly to my soul. I bought the book, sat on a bench, and pored over it. As it turns out, this book remains among the most influential I've ever read. The exact copy I purchased in the mall still sits on my shelf today.

Principle-Centered Leadership opened my eyes to the source of the problem I was having at work. I was focused on what I wanted people to know about me and how my ideas were the best innovations to grace this church since the arrival of pew cushions. I was not focusing on understanding my team members or others who were a part of the church. I was not having rewarding conversations because I was not listening. Honestly it had not even occurred to me to focus on understanding others.

Covey's perspective—"Seek first to understand"—turned my world upside down. "Only when you fully understand will you be able to be understood."[13] That advice has changed my view of conversations and relationships in all areas of my life: not just at work but with neighbors, friends, family, and even random conversational partners. Listening, empathy, and understanding don't come naturally to me. To this day, I have to fight against my instinct to get my perspective across in every conversation. But in my better moments, when the highest goal is to understand, my conversations almost always create a more meaningful connection with others.

It becomes even harder, and even more important, to seek understanding when the topic of conversation is contentious. Too frequently we convey our opinions and beliefs in black-or-white, all-or-nothing terms. Dr. Ling Dinse, chair of the social work department at Messiah University in Mechanicsburg, Pennsylvania, noticed her undergraduate students' growing difficulty in relating to those who held different views. They seemed to perceive differences as threats rather than opportunities to broaden their perspective or understanding.

As a researcher, Dinse began to explore the practice of having intentional, structured conversations with those who are different from us. She set up environments that helped students learn to listen, adapting guidelines provided by the nonprofit Living Room Conversations.

- Listen to understand, not to reply. Only ask follow-up questions to gain more clarity. Don't ask follow-up questions to challenge what another person has said. Simply seek to understand.

- Speak to be understood, not to persuade or correct someone. Don't speak for longer than you listen. Share the space to speak with others equally and only share more when others ask questions.

- Be authentic and welcome authenticity from others.

- Show respect and suspend judgment.[14]

Once given a safe space and some conversational guidelines, students showed marked improvement in their ability to connect with others and even critically evaluate their own presumptions.[15] Dinse's fascinating research validates the benefits derived from conversations with others who hold different perspectives and have vastly different lived experiences.

Author and commentator David Brooks explains how true conversation leads to understanding in his bestselling book *How to Know a Person.*

A lot of people think a good conversationalist is someone who can tell funny stories. That's a raconteur, but it's not a conversationalist. A lot of people think a good conversationalist is someone who can offer piercing insights on a range of topics. That's a lecturer, but not a conversationalist. A good conversationalist is a master of fostering a two-way exchange. A good conversationalist is capable of leading people on a mutual expedition toward understanding.[16]

While we can't control how others understand us, we can do much to understand others if we learn to listen with true curiosity. Every person's story, beliefs, and opinions are formed by their perspective and experiences, and we're always richer if we seek to understand, finding common ground and connection in ways we might never have imagined if we kept ourselves at the center of the conversation.

We might hear a great conversationalist say things and ask questions such as:

- "You mentioned you've been trying that new hobby. What drew you to it initially?"

- "That's a perspective I hadn't considered before. Could you help me understand what values, principles, or experiences are guiding your thinking?"

- "What was the highlight of your weekend? I'd love to hear what made it special for you."

- "I'm wondering if I've fully understood what you meant. Could I try to summarize what I think you're saying, and you can tell me if I've missed anything important?"

- "I'm curious about that recipe you used. Could you tell me more about how you learned to make it?"

- "I noticed you really lit up when talking about that book. What aspects of the story resonated with you?"

My (Phil's) dear friend Jeff Eberts recently passed away after a three-year battle with cancer. Jeff deeply embodied listening and engaging others with genuine curiosity. Over more than two decades of friendship, I experienced his skill as a conversationalist one-on-one and regularly observed his engagement with others. Jeff always gave his undivided attention in conversation. He was truly interested in getting to know people and appreciating who they were. His genuine desire to know others made him a natural in starting conversations and asking engaging questions. Jeff's questions were gentle and exploratory. "Tell me more" was a hallmark of his conversations, as were affirmations that communicated "you're special" and "you're valued."

Jeff wasn't quick with advice, stories that topped yours, or judgment. But he sure was quick with sincere care, affirmation, empathy, and grace. A few months before he passed away, I asked him about his conversational curiosity. He said, "I just love getting to know people. Everyone has a story, and most people love to share it, even if it is the surface-level bits and pieces. Actively listening to them gives me the opportunity to get to know and understand them better, and hopefully, it is also affirming to them. In a way, I sense God's presence as a person shares their story. It's privileged, even sacred, territory."[17]

Curiosity and Questions

Curiosity unlocks deeper communication. It invites us to set aside the need to be heard and immerse ourselves in the other person's experiences and reflections. Conversation flows easily when we're truly curious, asking questions, and wanting to know what the other person is interested in. Perhaps still more important, curiosity communicates care and empathy.

In her book *Brown Faces, White Spaces*, Latasha Morrison tells the story of a pivotal conversation she had in 2016 with Eric, a campus pastor of the Austin, Texas, church where she served on staff. Latasha was mourning the string of violent deaths of Black and Brown men that occurred in the months prior: Michael Brown, Alton Sterling, Philando Castile, and Micah Xavier Johnson. Though she was internally reeling, she accepted and expected that this would be a business-as-usual discussion. To her surprise, Eric began their meeting with a simple, sincere question: "How are you doing?"

> My emotions must have shown even though I was at a loss for words—a rare occurrence for me. Before I could come up with a meaningful response, he looked at me and said, "I have no words for what is happening. I'm so angry."
>
> His statement broke something loose in me. I felt seen. Understood. I found the words I needed to express my anger and frustration. As I spoke, both our eyes filled with tears. It occurred to me later that this powerful moment only occurred because Eric—a white man—made space for my pain.[18]

Eric's approach wasn't just kind and empathetic, it was profoundly biblical. Jesus, too, placed others at the center of his conversations by asking them questions. His questions were rooted in genuine interest or posed to carefully challenge another person's assumptions. By many accounts, there are more than 300 instances in the Gospels when Jesus asked a question. Interestingly, of the 183 recorded questions others asked of Jesus, he only answered three directly. How did he respond on each of the other 180 instances? Sometimes he told a parable or offered a cryptic remark, prompting the question asker to further reflection. Most often, he asked a question in return.[19]

Many years ago, I (Jeff) committed to becoming a good question asker so I could understand others better. For a few years it was nothing but hard work. I had to discipline myself to keep thinking about good questions to ask. During hard conversations, I had to force myself to assume I didn't understand the other person and keep seeking their point of view. But somewhere along the way, something shifted, and I developed a true sense of curiosity. Now I feel a sense of excitement and anticipation when I get to spend time with someone I don't know very well or have the opportunity for a more extended conversation.

I've also learned how easy it is to neglect that sense of curiosity with people I know well. I'm far too quick to assume I know what my wife is thinking or feeling. Instead of being curious about Christy's thoughts and feelings, I too hastily offer my two cents. I have this same tendency with close friends and coworkers; it's easy to assume I understand their perspective fully because I know them well. I continue to work to grow my curiosity with those I know best.

Brain research on processing information, making decisions, and responding to people around us points to the value of the approach Jesus modeled. Dr. David Rock's research indicates that when another person offers us advice—or even simply shares an opinion—our brains tend to interpret that as a threat. Conversely, our brains typically respond to a question in the opposite way (as long as the question isn't an attack in disguise, such as "Do you *really* think that?!"). Rather than viewing a question as a threat, our brains embrace it, almost as a reward. Pondering a question prompts synapses inside our brain to begin firing rapidly, making new connections.[20]

In his excellent book *The Art of Asking Better Questions*, J.R. Briggs offers practical advice for those who hope to have more Christlike conversations like the one Latasha and Eric shared. Briggs explains that our conversations falter because we don't move beyond asking for basic information. Great questions unlock powerful conversations by provoking thoughts and feelings and even inviting others (and ourselves) to greater vulnerability. He offers these helpful examples of how to "level up" to better questions:[21]

Common question	Next-level question
How are you?	What's been the most interesting part of your day thus far?
Where did you grow up?	What was the best part of where you grew up?
Where did you attend college?	What were your most formative experiences in college?
How was your vacation?	What was the most exciting experience or meaningful memory from your recent vacation?
Where do you work?	What are you currently working on that you're finding interesting or deeply satisfying?
Where do you live?	How might you describe your neighborhood in three adjectives?
What do you do for a living?	How did you end up doing what you do for a living?
How was your Father's Day?	What's the most meaningful part of being a father?
What do you like to do for fun?	If you had an entire Saturday with no responsibilities whatsoever on the calendar, what would you want to do?

Questions, shared from a posture of true care and curiosity, lead to some of our most powerful connections with others.

Doing Life Side by Side

Tjarks's true purpose in writing of his small group wasn't simply to recount an experience that went from weird to rewarding but because in his life, conversation was the beginning of something David Brooks calls it "accompaniment"—doing life side by side.[22] Tjarks was writing after a diagnosis of terminal cancer. He didn't know how much time he had left (months, it turned out), but he knew what it was like to be raised without a father, and it was "the one thing that [he] never wanted" for his son, who was just two years old at the time. He titled the article, which expressed his hopes that this community would continue to accompany his family through life, "Does My Son Know You?" Tjarks never knew his father's friends, who tapered off over the years his dad battled Parkinson's disease.

"I don't want Jackson to have the same childhood that I did," he wrote. "I want him to wonder why his dad's friends always come over and shoot hoops with him. Why they always invite him to their houses. Why there are so many of them at his games. I hope that he gets sick of them."[23] Though these terms are ours, not his, Tjarks hoped they would show up as *ezers*, ready to help, and that this *koinōnia* community would have more than enough resources among it to teach his son to grill burgers, fix a car, and tie a tie as they lived out the kind of community God intended. He hoped that what started as simple conversation would end up as something extraordinary.

Not every conversation will end in something extraordinary. Some will be dull, others infuriating, most utterly ordinary. But talking with one another is where accompaniment and extraordinary outcomes start.

When I (Jeff) think about how most of my closest friendships developed, in retrospect, I can see a million little conversations that fostered our connection. I shared in a previous chapter the desire that Christy and I have to grow closer to our neighbors, and I'm thankful we have a foundation of friendship to build on as we invest more intentionally. But here's what's interesting: The friendships we've built so far have been established through dozens of chats as we're coming and going or pausing from yard work to catch up and share family news. Just the everyday chatter kind of stuff. Conversation is paving the way for deeper connection.

Similarly, I've become quite good friends with Michael, whom I met in a Work Life course facilitated by RestoreOKC. The class is for men and women who are underemployed or unemployed and seeking skills, relationships, and experiences that will unlock more significant employment opportunities. I got paired with Michael in the class, and my role was to be his ally as he worked through the program. Soon we started hanging out after class, grabbing tacos or a hamburger, and that's where the good stuff happened. I know all about his love life, his granddaughter, the tragedy of losing his mom, and his battle with addiction. He knows all about my love for kayaking, my new grandkids, a few of my personal struggles, and some of my favorite books that I've read over the last few years. When we chat about this stuff, we're building a meaningful bond.

Accompaniment is an essential ingredient to *ezer* (one to another), *allēlōn* (to each other), and *koinōnia* (each to all), and talking with one another—in particular when our conversations are shaped by a curious posture—is an essential ingredient to accompaniment. It is also core to who we are. In Genesis 3, after sinning against God, Adam and Eve hide. Genesis 3:9 tells us, "But the LORD God called to the man, 'Where are you?'" God was used to hanging out with Adam and Eve, conversing with them, as part of his perfect design. When sin severed that connection, we can infer that God missed walking and talking with them. Right there, in our creation story, we find the idea of accompaniment and conversation as a bridge to connection.

Jesus was Emmanuel—God with us, God accompanying us in the flesh. Jesus invested his life in relationships with his disciples, spending hours each day with them and sustaining that pattern for years (Luke 8:1; John 15:15). The disciples did the same, leaving all else behind to follow Jesus. Likewise, the compelling stories of the early church in Acts emphasize time spent together: eating, worshiping, serving, praying, and simply doing life in community over a period of weeks, months, and years (Acts 2:42-47; 20:7-12).

In many cases, our closest and most meaningful relationships— those best-suited to address the loneliness epidemic—will unfold over months, years, or even decades. Our time in conversation may look different in different seasons, but accompaniment has more to do with lifestyle than life stage: We may host others in our homes, simply show up in response to an invitation, schedule time for a phone call, or even engineer errands to coincide. The path to deeper relationships begins with accompanying one another.

We aren't sure who wrote the book of Hebrews, but we know that the author had a personal relationship with Jesus' first disciples and a front-row seat to observe the practices that helped the early followers of Jesus form *koinōnia* communities. The writer of Hebrews offers this guidance: "Let us consider how we may spur one another on toward love and good deeds, not giving up meeting together, as some are in the habit of doing, but encouraging one another—and all the more as you see the Day approaching" (Hebrews 10:24-25).

It's easy to "give up meeting together" in a world with so many proxies for proximity. We can capture glimpses into our friends' lives as spectators through social media or even join church from our couch. These technologies weren't available during Jesus' time, so we have no direct insight into how he would have applied them. But we can observe that Jesus' life placed an exclamation point on face-to-face proximity and engagement.

For the sake of convenience and efficiency, Jesus could have locked himself away penning wise words and instruction manuals for life—and they would have been incredible. He could have adopted the common practice of important leaders of his day, having assistants schedule meetings at his office—*the Rabbi will see you now*—for those who wanted to come, talk, and seek his counsel. But Jesus was committed to accompanying people.

We think of Jesus traveling into dangerous territory to be with Martha and Mary after his friend and their brother, Lazarus, had died (John 11). Jesus didn't have to be there to heal Lazarus. In fact, just a few chapters earlier, John 4 recounts the story of a miraculous long-distance healing. The miracle didn't necessitate Jesus' physical presence, but his commitment to accompany Mary, Martha, and Lazarus did.

The passage in Hebrews speaks not only to the value of our time together—don't give it up!—but also to the use of that time. We are to stir each other up and encourage one another. Our casual conversations and time together, worthwhile and important in their own right, ought to be opening the door for deeper conversations and a life of accompaniment.

While many of us have conversations about our faith, we do so less often than ever,[24] and many cite a desire to avoid "tension or arguments" or fears of offending others as a reason not to engage.[25] But if we are committed to the Great Commission and truly believe that Christ-centered communities are the answer to the loneliness epidemic, we need to be sharing far more of life and conversation. Talking about our faith—something many consider deeply personal as well as potentially inflammatory—can be intimidating, but faith doesn't have to be a conversation-stopper or a relational roadblock.

My (Jeff's) friend Nate lived in Tunisia for a time, where less than 1 percent of the population is Christian. He worked at a climbing gym and a consulting firm, and, as God prompted, he would ask his colleagues and new friends, "Have you ever known a Christian?" Because Christians were so few and far between, most would say no. "Well, I'm a Christian," Nate would respond. "Do you have any questions for me?" Rather than telling others what he thought they needed to know, Nate allowed them to guide faith conversations. His posture of humility and vulnerability opened the door to significant, life-changing conversations with those he was privileged to accompany for a season.

We think the writer of Hebrews would affirm this approach. Accompanying. Listening. Asking and inviting questions. Being curious. Challenging each other's assumptions. Talking to one another is simple but utterly transformative. Our lives, and the lives of those around us, will be more joyful, abundant, and contented only to the degree that we are not alone.

We have to be together, in conversation, to live the life that Jesus has called us to live and that he modeled for us. Let's not go with the cultural current and spend ever-increasing time by ourselves; instead, let's make a concerted effort to dive into conversation with the people around us. Let's chat it up with our neighbors. Let's take out the earbuds on lunch break and converse with a coworker. Let's call a friend when we go for a walk and chat. Let's grab coffee or dinner and make space for good conversation. Let's see conversation as the most foundational tool to accompany one another.

Designing a Life of Talking with One Another

Slow down to chat. Create margin for conversation. Build it into your schedule through the day and throughout the week. See conversation as one of the most valuable investments you can make with your time.

Master the basics of good conversation. David Brooks gives practical guidance we can follow, starting today. We highly recommend his book *How to Know a Person: The Art of Seeing Others Deeply and Being Deeply Seen,* but we'll highlight a few relevant suggestions here.

- Treat attention as an on/off switch, not a dimmer. Our brains process information much faster than a person can speak, so it's natural for our minds to wander in a conversation. Resist that tendency and fully pay attention with your mind, posture, and eye contact.

- Be a loud listener. Listen actively. Respond with nods and changes in your expression. Keep eye contact. Occasionally, restate what you hear the other person saying to ensure you understand it.

- Don't fear the pause. It's okay to allow a bit of silence as you reflect on what a person is saying. Resist the urge to constantly fill the air with more words. Take an extra breath and let the other person know you're thoughtfully reflecting on what they've shared.

- Loop back. When someone says something important, respond with, "What I hear you saying is . . ." to ensure you hear both the information and the other person's intent. This kind of looping back helps us listen more intentionally.

- Don't be a topper. If someone tells you about an experience or problem they are facing, resist the urge to respond by sharing how you've experienced the same thing.[26]

Discover the power of questions. Jesus was a master of conversation. He already knew what others were thinking and feeling, but as an act of love, he talked with them. The Gospel writers portrayed

Jesus as someone tuned in to others' thoughts, feelings, and beliefs. John 3 tells the story of Jesus meeting with Nicodemus in the quiet of the night to discuss his deep questions. Jesus patiently listened, asked thought-provoking questions, and carefully challenged Nicodemus. One chapter later (John 4), John recounts Jesus' effort to connect with the Samaritan woman through heartfelt conversation. Throughout all the Gospels, we see Jesus talking, listening, sharing stories, challenging, encouraging, and exhorting.

- Ask open-ended questions. The best conversation-enriching questions begin with words like "How did you . . . ?" "What is it like . . . ?" or "Could you tell me about . . . ?" Avoid questions that sound judgmental or can be answered with a simple yes or no.

- Go four questions deep. Don't stop with the first question. Ask a follow-up to learn more or understand better, then ask a third and a fourth question. This is a practical way to keep curiosity flowing and dial back our tendency to assume we understand what the other person is saying.

- Ask questions about things people love to talk about. Connect around interests or experiences the other person enjoys. Ask many questions about their interests and seek to understand more about what is important to them.

- Ask for more details when a person is sharing something. When we share an experience, we tend to leave out many details that seem obvious to us. Keep asking for more details to help a person get their full perspective out.

Make the most of opportunities for conversation. The Living Room Conversations website (livingroomconversations.org) provides practical ways to get a conversation going in many different settings. This resource and many others like it will help you plan great questions to discuss at your next small group meeting, work activity, or gathering of friends.

Reflect Individually

- The American Time Use Survey indicates that Americans spend more time alone each year. How have you experienced this in your own life and relationships?

- What do you enjoy most about having meaningful conversations with others? What aspects of conversing are more challenging for you?

- How could you open yourself up to converse with someone who might be feeling overlooked today? Or if you're feeling overlooked, how could you signal to someone else that you're open to conversation?

- What ideas from "Designing a Life of Talking with One Another" are relevant to you? How could you put one or two of these ideas into action?

Discuss Together

- How much do we enjoy conversing with people who are different from us? When these opportunities have come our way in the past, how have we responded?

- What can we learn from Jesus' conversations and example of life in community? What would it look like to model our approach to community and conversation after Jesus'?

- How could our community be richer and more joyful if we listened more, asked more questions, and had deeper conversations with one another?

6

WELCOME ONE ANOTHER

Then Jesus said to his host, "When you give a luncheon or dinner, do not invite your friends, your brothers or sisters, your relatives, or your rich neighbors; if you do, they may invite you back and so you will be repaid. But when you give a banquet, invite the poor, the crippled, the lame, the blind, and you will be blessed."

LUKE 14:12-14

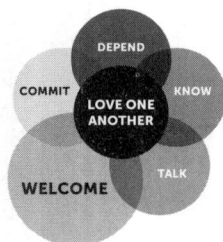

FOLLOWING THE RELEASE OF Trevor Noah's memoir *Born a Crime*, the comedian and former host of *The Daily Show* described his struggle with aloneness to journalist Lesley Stahl on *60 Minutes.* Noah grew up in South Africa, where his Black mother and White father's interracial relationship was illegal under the system of apartheid. Neither light-skinned enough to resemble his father nor dark-skinned enough to resemble his mother, Noah recalls, "All I wanted to do was belong."[1]

The feeling of not belonging continues to overshadow Noah. Wealth, success, and fame haven't dispelled it because wealth and fame aren't restitution for the loss of dignity that Noah experienced as a kid. It doesn't take an egregious system like apartheid to rob people of dignity. Any kind of marginalization can do it, and we cannot underestimate how many people in our towns, neighborhoods, and cities feel the way Noah does.

Research and data analytics firm YouGov developed the Belonging Barometer to understand how well people feel they belong. This tool assumes a person's feeling of belonging increases the more they

- feel emotionally connected.

- are welcomed and included.

- perceive they are able to influence decision-making.

- feel able to be their whole and authentic self.

- are valued as a person and for their contributions.

- are in relationships that are as satisfying as they want them to be.

- feel like an insider who understands how the environment works.

- feel comfortable expressing their opinions.

- are treated equally.

- feel that they "truly belong."[2]

By these standards, 64 percent of Americans say they don't feel they belong in their workplace, 68 percent say they don't belong in our nation, and 74 percent feel they don't belong in their local community. Perhaps worse, nearly 20 percent of Americans don't report belonging *anywhere*, in any area of their life.[3]

It's easy to convince ourselves that we don't make others feel this way. After all, we're not working to prop up an oppressive system like apartheid or even knowingly excluding anyone. But unless we are intentionally inclusive and welcoming, exclusion is the default. Let's zoom in on our daily lives.

An Invisible Hand

In the digital world, complex algorithms designed to predict and pique our interest constantly push us toward the familiar. While searching for a podcast recommended by a friend, I (Jeff) recently discovered an entirely new ecosystem of podcasts focused on ideas I'd never heard about! Some are wildly popular, with tens of thousands of five-star ratings, but because my podcast app algorithm knows what I typically listen to, it serves up recommendations of similar content. Echo chambers are always on offer, but I have to intentionally seek out diverse perspectives. The app has no idea that I'd love to gain perspectives from people who see and think very differently from me.

We experience this same kind of sorting where we live.[4] Unless we purposely do otherwise, we tend to rent or buy homes in areas where people in similar social and economic demographics also live. This "sorting" was still quite invisible to me when my wife and I purchased our last home a decade ago, but over the past ten years it has proven true that, with few exceptions, our neighbors are much like us. In a very real sense this is a sort of segregation happening right under our noses, but we don't see it happening because we're in the middle of it. To build friendships with people who are different from us in significant ways, we have to intentionally spend time in other areas of our city.

In both the physical and the digital world, it seems as though an invisible hand is sorting us to be with others like us, often without our knowledge or assent. A subtle current pulls us toward people, ideas, and perspectives that are familiar. We feel safe in these cocoons of similarity where we're confident of our standing, connection, and belonging.

We Like People Who Are Like Us

Researchers conducting one of the most extensive field studies on friendship formation found that the bigger the pool of potential friends, the more selective we become in finding those who share our values, attitudes, and perspectives. A study from Wellesley College and the University of Kansas revealed that from the moment we meet a new person, we begin to self-select. The level of similarity between two individuals likely determines whether or not a friendship develops. "You try to create a social world where you're comfortable, where you succeed, where you have people you can trust and with whom you can cooperate to meet your goals," explains professor of psychology and co-lead researcher Chris Crandall.[5]

None of this is intentional inhospitableness, but we can see these behaviors in ourselves every day. Walking through our office hallways, we stop to chat with people we know and those with whom we regularly collaborate. When we attend a church service, we sit in the same area each week and engage with the same handful of people. These interactions feel comfortable and predictable and we, like everyone else, default toward comfort and predictability. We're not excluding others on purpose, but we're certainly not engaging others with intentionality. It's just that we like people who like us, and we like to be with people who are like us! It makes us wonder how many, like Noah, feel more left out than we realize.

Becca and I (Phil) spent five years trying to establish friendships at one church in a new city. In many ways we were "insiders." We shared the beliefs and demographics of our fellow congregants, but even so, we couldn't "break in." We never experienced the mutuality of *allēlōn* (to each other). Conversations frequently circled back to, "Remember when . . . ?" and, of course, we and any other relative newcomer didn't. We hadn't been there "when," and over the course of time, we began to feel we weren't truly wanted there now either.

The "remember whens" served as constant, subtle reinforcement of in-groups and out-groups. Without intentional effort, our churches' "close-knit communities" can be notoriously unwelcoming places.

Author and Benedictine sister Joan Chittister offers further insight into why we do this. When every interaction activates either a sense of threat or reward, "Sameness becomes a kind of security blanket that wraps us up in the warm feeling of being acceptable to the groups with which we identify and whose approval we seek," she says. "We are safe because we are just like everybody else. To be socially acceptable we have allowed ourselves to become socially invisible."[6] But we cannot simultaneously be invisible and inclusive, so we'll have to choose. To welcome others is to risk something, and the way of Jesus challenges us not to get stuck in our safe and predictable ways.

In fact, one of Jesus' most well-known teachings makes it clear there is a future payoff when we go out of our way to be an *ezer* to people in very different circumstances, expressing love one to another. Jesus tells us that those who care for others in such a way will hear his Father say,

> Take your inheritance, the kingdom prepared for you since the creation of the world. For I was hungry and you gave me something to eat, I was thirsty and you gave me something to drink, I was a stranger and you invited me in, I needed clothes and you clothed me, I was sick and you looked after me, I was in prison and you came to visit me. (Matthew 25:34-36)

God's desires for our relationships are so different from ours!

An Expansive Welcome

The four Gospel writers shared so many stories that portray Jesus going out of his way to cross social, ideological, racial, and gender barriers to extend friendship to people who might otherwise have been ignored or "othered." Welcoming others is an unmistakable aspect of the upside-down way of living that Jesus taught and modeled.

We saw it with the Samaritan woman at the well. While most Jews summarily avoided Samaria because of centuries of bad blood between the two groups, Jesus went right through it. As a man, it was taboo for Jesus to address a woman individually, but he didn't just talk to this woman, he made her the first to know who he truly was: the Messiah, God's Son (John 4).

Jesus went out of his way to create belonging between himself and the woman at the well. He acted as though he belonged with her and made her feel she belonged with him. She was different from him in every way, yet he made her feel accepted and welcomed as part of his community with no strings attached, regardless of race, gender, or reputation.

We can see the same principle at work earlier in Jesus' life when he called his twelve disciples. In Matthew's list of the Twelve, three disciples warrant an extra description: Judas, who betrayed Jesus; Matthew, the tax collector; and Simon, the Zealot (Matthew 10:2-4). We can't help believing that Matthew recorded these descriptors for a reason! Perhaps it is because, based on these brief descriptions, Matthew and Simon would have been like oil and water. Matthew compromised to appease Rome, while Simon fought to overthrow Roman rule. They likely would have viewed each other with contempt and hostility. Jesus showed us there's room at his table for those of different beliefs, backgrounds, and lifestyles.

As his descriptor indicates, Simon probably belonged to the Zealot movement, a Jewish nationalist movement that opposed Roman occupation. Zealots were known for their fierce loyalty to their homeland and resistance to Roman rule. They were also known for expressing that resistance through violence. Jesus called Simon at a time when his life was sharply opposed to what Jesus would teach in the Sermon on the Mount. In the beginning, Simon's ways didn't look a lot like Jesus' ways, yet Jesus recognized Simon's potential and invited him to a new way of understanding.

As a tax collector, Matthew would have struggled to belong. The Jews thought he was a sellout because he chose to profit from the Roman Empire's control over the Jews, and Rome looked down on him because he was a Jew. Because of who he was and what he did, there was nowhere Matthew was fully welcome, until Jesus invited him in. Jesus could have met Matthew at the market, in a synagogue, or anywhere, but Scripture tells us Matthew was sitting at his tax collector's booth when Jesus called him (Matthew 9:9). That setting communicates so much. Matthew never had to wonder if Jesus knew what kind of person he *really* was or if he needed to clean up his act before coming to Jesus. Jesus knew exactly who Matthew was, and Jesus said he belonged.

After Matthew responded to Jesus' invitation to follow him, Jesus joined him for dinner in his home. This wasn't a private chat where Matthew and Jesus discussed the conditions of his welcome: It was more like a dinner party, where fellow tax collectors and "sinners" showed up too. The religious leaders who looked on were appalled, but Jesus responded that he hadn't come for those who think they're already healthy but for those who know they're sick (Matthew 9:10-13).

Not only did Jesus welcome both Simon and Matthew, he led them to accept and love each other. The Gospels don't record any direct interaction between Simon and Matthew, but we can infer a lot from the fact that they spent the majority of their lives together for the three years of Jesus' public ministry and possibly even beyond as they continued their work to advance the gospel.

They were also among those present with Jesus at the Last Supper when he prayed that his disciples gathered in that room, as well as his future followers, would be known for their unity and love for one another.

The Center Is Jesus

In the book *The Shaping of Things to Come*, authors Michael Frost and Alan Hirsch elaborate on missiologist Paul Hiebert's idea of bounded sets versus centered sets: two different ways to envision belonging in Christ's kingdom.[7] In a bounded set, members are determined by focusing on the boundary, like horses inside a corral. A fence clearly delineates which horses belong to a particular rancher. In a bounded set, the focus is on whether someone is inside or outside the fence, concentrating not on movement but position. The key question is, Who's in, and who's out? We've observed that bounded-set communities tend to keep to themselves, fearful of being perceived by others as outside the boundaries.

A centered set, in contrast, has no walls, fences, or dividing lines. There's no boundary to keep people out, but there is something compelling at the center to draw them in. In a centered set, belonging looks more like a watering hole than a corral. At any given moment, an animal might be moving either away from or toward the watering hole, and the focus is on whether the movement is toward or away from the center. We've observed that people in centered-set communities tend to feel more free to look outward and welcome others into their community.

Pastor and author John Ortberg reflects,

If we focus on Jesus as the center, then the key question becomes whether someone is oriented toward him or away from him. We realize that God is in a much better position than we are to know who's in and who's out. We also realize that everyone has something to learn, that everyone has a next step to take, and we don't have to make ourselves seem more different than we really are. We embrace our common humanity.

Ortberg continues,

If we treat Christianity as a bounded set, there will always be a disconnect between the gospel and discipleship. The gospel will be presented as something to get you "inside the circle." . . . However, if we treat Christianity as a centered set, the relationship between the gospel and discipleship becomes much clearer.[8]

Are there differences between those who've more fully aligned their lives with the way of Jesus and others who are only beginning to show interest in following Jesus? Of course there are. But our focus on Jesus as the center creates the common ground we need to welcome anyone who wants to move toward Jesus. It is part of our calling as Christ's followers to make others feel they belong, are safe, and are accepted, just as he did.

Jesus gave shape and color to the concept of belonging:

- He created an emotional connection with others (John 11:35).

- He made others feel able to be their whole and authentic self (Luke 19:1-10).

- He treated every person interested in him like an insider (Matthew 5:3-12).

- He gave people a sense of autonomy (Matthew 4:18-22).

- He treated people equally and made them feel welcome (John 4:1-42).

The "Smokers' Porch"

Jesus shows us the art of being inclusive, caring, and loving toward others while also knowing and adhering to God's intentions for humanity. It is possible to do both. Church communities that welcome others as Jesus did make space for people to belong even before they believe. We've seen through the stories of savings groups that genuine transformation happens through relationships and in community.

Yet welcoming those who don't share our lifestyle or beliefs to find a home in our church communities—attending worship services, serving in the church, joining a small group—feels uncomfortable. One person commented candidly to us, "The struggle for me is when I feel I have to embrace the lifestyle or actions of others as acceptable, even if it goes against what I feel is biblical. Is the point to love each other and turn a blind eye to the lifestyle?"

To Josef, who pastors a church in Lancaster, Pennsylvania, a porch where some attendees gather to smoke before or after services has become a powerful symbol of welcome. When questioned by a congregant if it was appropriate for a church to have a "smokers' porch," Pastor Josef simply replied, "I hope there's always a smokers' porch, and I hope it's always full."

For Josef, making room for the porch isn't really about smoking. It's about living out the message boldly painted across the church's façade: "a church for all people." There's no disqualifying belief, lifestyle, or appearance. The porch is simply another threshold of transformation in a community where people are welcomed to come just as they are, and—in experiencing the transforming love of Jesus through *ezer, allēlōn,* and *koinōnia*—may not always stay as they are.

Regardless of belief, background, or behavior, Josef's church affirms that everyone deserves a place to belong. "We want to invite people to come, just as they are, and be part of us. We don't want them to have to change their behavior and then come."[9] The church has a centered-set mindset—focusing not on maintaining boundaries between "insiders" and "outsiders" but instead creating a community centered on Christ that draws people toward transformation through belonging.

We suspect those who had already been called as Jesus' disciples felt displeased, irritated, and confused when he welcomed Matthew the tax collector and Simon the Zealot to become a part of his community of followers. They probably felt it again when they watched from a short distance as Jesus chatted midday with the Samaritan woman, drank from her bucket, and invited her to feel she belonged. We're right there with the disciples in experiencing some discomfort when we reflect on how Jesus made "outsiders" feel welcomed.

But we must remember that God has welcomed *all of us*. The apostle Paul writes in Romans 5:8, "While we were still sinners, Christ died for us." When we're tempted to question who we ought to welcome, we remember Paul's words in 1 Timothy 1:15, "Here is a trustworthy saying that deserves full acceptance: Christ Jesus came into the world to save sinners—of whom I am the worst." Like Paul, we marvel that God has welcomed us. When we remember that we have been welcomed, it changes how we welcome others. If we remembered that Jesus' friendship to us preceded any change within us, would that deepen our desire to welcome others who see or act differently than us?

Welcoming Strangers

One church-sponsored savings group we visited in southern Malawi operated in a Muslim-majority context. Generally Christians and Muslims in the area remained separate, living as strangers, but savings group members from the church invited their Muslim neighbors to join them in this endeavor. The group didn't stop praying, reading the Bible, or worshiping together, but they warmly welcomed their fellow community members. They've lovingly begun to refer to each other as "cousins" in their faith, recognizing their very real differences while allowing for a sense of belonging together.

When it comes to welcoming strangers, my (Jeff's) friend Annette inspires me. Following the fall of Kabul, Afghanistan, in 2021, Annette heard the news that more than one thousand Afghans would be moving to Oklahoma City as part of the Afghan Placement and Assistance program. Annette has a lot of rich experience but no experience in caring for refugees. This was well outside her comfort zone, yet Annette took the initiative to contact a local refugee resettlement agency and receive training as a volunteer so she could be matched with an Afghan family.

For several years, she has walked alongside a family of seven as they've found a new home and jobs, enrolled in school, navigated complex systems, and confronted language barriers. She's cheered on the Thunder (our local NBA team) alongside these new friends and been the person they could call with questions or in crisis. It's been both rewarding and challenging. At times Annette has felt overwhelmed with their need for guidance and assistance with appointments, job searches, and seemingly endless piles of paperwork. She's struggled with guilt when she couldn't be available to help or when she enjoyed privileges they couldn't afford.

Cultural differences have also created unexpected challenges. Brief visits have extended into hours-long hospitality rituals. Annette has had to carefully navigate the delicate balance of integrating the family into her social circles and church community while respecting their different religious beliefs and maintaining appropriate boundaries. She has been an *ezer* (consistently demonstrating God's love one to another), but that's never an easy task, and in this case it's been complicated by the trauma the family has endured and the vastly different culture to which they are adapting.

Annette loves Jesus, and she doesn't know if this family ever will, but she rightly recognizes that their faith has no bearing on her call to welcome others, even when it's inconvenient or difficult.

Jesus Awakens Our Imagination

I (Jeff) recently reconnected with Matt, a longtime friend who lives in my city. We enjoy spending time together, talking about our work, learning from each other, and encouraging one another, so we established a standing coffee meeting every month or so. Several meetings in, our conversation began to venture into territory that revealed vast differences in our perspectives. As we pressed into the discussion, it became clear that we both strongly hold to some ideas that feel and seem incompatible. With this dawning realization, I could feel emotion and a desire to challenge Matt's assumptions welling up inside of me.

As I listened to my friend, I flashed back to a breakout session that a colleague and I facilitated a few months prior during Life.Church's yearly staff gathering. The topic was "Unity in Our Differences," and our beautifully diverse team revisited how the example of Jesus has enabled us to appreciate our differences while remaining unified in our relationships as a team and as a church more broadly.

Mid-conversation with Matt, my thoughts returned to one of the main points from our session: It's easy to fixate on people's opinions rather than opening our hearts to their stories. In our families, workplaces, and communities, tensions around differing political or ideological views can prompt conflict or avoidance. Rather than extending a warm welcome or pursuing a deeper understanding, we're drawn to take sides, gravitating toward groups where certainty feels safe and familiar. Yet those who foster true belonging recognize that beneath every viewpoint are hopes, fears, and dreams—each worthy of understanding. I felt God's prompt to stop building the invisible wall that I had begun erecting between us.

As we've seen, Jesus entered into a society sorted into rigid groups—the privileged Sadducees, rule-driven Pharisees, withdrawn Essenes, and revolutionary Zealots. Instead of reinforcing these divisions, he awakened people's imagination to something far greater. He showed us what relationships with people who see the world in very different ways could look like when they're marked by compassion, love, and grace.

As I sat listening to my friend, I silently prayed that I'd be able to adopt that imagination Jesus calls us to seek right there in that moment. I focused on asking Matt questions about how his perspective evolved, seeking to understand the struggles, joys, and pivot points that shaped his views. My main goal in that moment was to walk away from the conversation feeling closer to my friend despite the differences in our political viewpoints. And that is exactly what happened. As I intentionally listened with genuine care, my perspectives softened and expanded, creating a space where connection could flourish despite our differences. We still meet every month, we talk about our differences, and our friendship has never been stronger.

Designing Our Lives to Welcome Others

We are not naive; welcoming and building friendships with people different from us is difficult and pulls us outside of our comfort zone. But it is what Jesus did, and if we want to chip away at the problem of aloneness in our world, it will take a long-term, intentional posture of welcoming one another.

Creating spaces of welcome is an essential Christian practice, and it is good for us as well as others. Through their research, the creators of the Belonging Barometer found that, paradoxically, wanting to get to know others who are different is directly connected to feeling a sense of belonging. In other words, our own sense of belonging increases as we seek friendships with those who are different from us![10]

Chris Crandall, the co-lead researcher on the Wellesley College/University of Kansas friendship study writes,

> Friends are for comfort, taking it easy, relaxing, not being challenged—and those are good things. But you can't have only that need. You also need new ideas, people to correct you when you're loony. If you hang out only with people who are loony like you, you can be out of touch with the big, beautiful, diverse world.[11]

As Christians, our discipleship journey is played out in community in a big, beautiful, diverse world. Proverbs 27:17 talks about iron sharpening iron. Hebrews 10:24 instructs us to "spur one another on toward love and good deeds." And Colossians 3:16 says to "teach and admonish one another." But without differing perspectives, it becomes very hard to obey these commands. Monolithic communities will miss out on opportunities to grow in Christlikeness.

Both literally and figuratively, those who share the same perspective or viewing angle will share the same blind spots. Who can most easily identify our blind spots? *People who don't share our perspective.* People whose life experiences or personal traits offer a different viewing angle on our situation. God's kingdom is diverse, by design, and we need that diversity in our lives and faith communities.

As with all the other one-anothers we've proposed, we have to design our lives differently to welcome others. There are a number of ways to begin to escape the default.

Examine your life. So much exclusion happens automatically and unintentionally. A first step might be to simply become aware of how we default toward those like us as we go about a typical day. Ask yourself how you were impacted by "the invisible hand" today. Humbly reflect on your implicit biases. Ask, "Why do I feel this way? What ideas shape my perception of a group of people who are different from me? What assumptions am I carrying? What are some of the ideas that form these stereotypes?"

Read new sources. Try reading a news source that's traditionally favored by those of a different theological or political persuasion. Read books or listen to podcasts that espouse viewpoints different from your own. We can grow in our understanding of other perspectives on current events when we intentionally expose ourselves to new information or look at the same information through a new lens.

Educate yourself. Begin to educate yourself on the challenging realities of life in your community or country for members of a different group: Whether it's those living below the poverty line, those of a different race, those who emigrated from another country, etc., our empathy will grow as our understanding grows.

Ask others to share their story. Look for opportunities to ask someone to share more of their story with you, especially when you meet someone who comes from a background or holds views dissimilar to your own. Listen to understand how their life experiences have shaped them. Before contributing your own perspectives or opinions on a point of contention, try respectfully asking something like, "Could you share how you came to that understanding?"

Release the burden of transformation. Remember that welcoming others doesn't mean we're responsible for changing their hearts, minds, or behaviors. We can release the pressure to convince, correct, or convert. When we approach others without an agenda to fix or change them, we free ourselves from fear and defensiveness. This posture allows us to trust that the Holy Spirit is already at work in ways we cannot see. Our calling is to welcome warmly. The work of transformation belongs to God.

Gather around food. There's something profound about the way food breaks down barriers, whether it's a cup of coffee, a meal in your home, or dinner at a restaurant. Eating together creates common ground and makes it easier to converse with people despite our differences. Somehow invisible barriers tend to fade when we pass plates and enjoy our favorite foods together.

Become conscious of "circle" posture. Author Glennon Doyle gave some advice to women that we'd like to extend to all followers of Christ: Form U's rather than circles. Circles feel warm and cozy to those on the inside—but there's always someone on the outside.

> If you are standing . . . in a circle and there is a woman standing alone in your circle's vicinity, the thing to do is: Notice her, smile at her, move over a bit, and say, "Hi, come join us!" Even if she decides not to join your circle—even if she looks at you like you're crazy—inviting her is still the thing to do. I mean this both with our literal circles . . . and our figurative circles. Let's widen our circles. Let's stand—and live—in horseshoes.[12]

Guard against unintended cliques. Building on the "circle" posture, be sensitive to the unintended exclusion that closer, long-standing friendships can create. For those newer to our group (whether church, work, or community), conversations about past relational experiences can contribute to a sense of exclusion or hierarchy in the group. A better way to approach these reminiscences is to engage the newer person in the story or experience, sharing it with them directly so they become an active recipient of the story rather than a passive bystander to our conversation. (By all means, if we find ourselves regularly gravitating to "remember way back when . . ." it's worth considering whether our posture/heart is truly welcoming.)

Sit in a different seat at church this Sunday. In certain churches, this suggestion would feel almost sacrilegious, but contrary to popular belief, churches don't have assigned seating. Move to a different seat and strike up a conversation with someone you don't yet know. Do more than just say hi; share your name and make a point to remember theirs.

Be open to disruption. These small steps are a vital beginning to welcoming others, but they likely aren't the end. Pray about what disruptive design choice God might be inviting you to embrace. It could be:

- Opening your home to a child in foster care
- Taking a family new to your community under your wing
- Establishing a close friendship with someone very different from you

God is infinitely more creative than we are, so ask him, "What would it look like for me to welcome others as you have welcomed me?"

Reflect Individually

- How do you connect with people who are different from you?
- Take a few minutes to read the story of Jesus and the Samaritan woman in John 4. What do you see Jesus doing or saying that you could emulate in your everyday life as you interact with others?
- Who do you know who would benefit from a greater sense of belonging? What could you do to connect with that person?

Discuss Together

- Before we knew each other, what differences might have kept us from becoming friends?

- How can we maintain unity in our group and community without expecting uniformity? How have we seen our group or other groups doing this well?

- Looking back through the "Designing Our Lives to Welcome Others" section of the chapter, what ideas stand out as relevant to our group? How will we put those ideas into practice?

7

COMMIT TO ONE ANOTHER

*This is how we know what love is: Jesus Christ
laid down his life for us. And we ought to lay
down our lives for our brothers and sisters.*

1 JOHN 3:16

JUST OUT OF COLLEGE, I (Phil) began my career journey on the sales force of a Fortune 200 company focused on providing business solutions to companies large and small. My on-the-job training taught me to uncover and highlight a prospect's problems and point to our product as the solution. "The patient has to understand how sick they are before they'll take action to get better," the logic went. We learned that the primary question in every potential customer's mind is WIIFM: "What's in it for me?" Answer that question compellingly and watch as doors open, rapport grows, and products sell! This strategy worked then and, although I'm no longer in sales, I'm convinced it would work just as well today.

Consumers worldwide want to know what's in it for them. Moreover, they want not only a great product but also a rewarding consumer experience, characterized by choice, convenience,

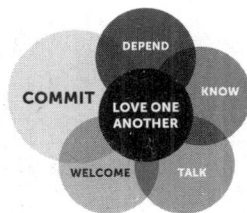

efficiency, and ease. According to one survey from the National Retail Federation, 97 percent of respondents indicated they had abandoned a purchase over lack of convenience.[1] Sometimes we just aren't all that committed.

I'm a big fan of one-click shopping, and as someone who hastily and joylessly careens down the grocery store aisles, it's been suggested that I'm best-suited to curbside pickup. It's easy to see how these little choices can push us toward isolation (as often the most "convenient" option involves little to no human interaction), but the far more pernicious problem arises when our consumer mindset seeps into our relationships. Consumerism and the pursuit of convenience are fundamentally at odds with commitment. And while we may hesitate to commit, commitment is essential to loving one another in the way of Jesus.

Inconvenient (Divine) Interruptions

Of all the one-anothers, commitment may be the least popular. It's not just that it makes demands—it tends to make them at the most inconvenient times. We don't get to choose when a loved one falls ill, a crisis hits our church, or a friendship needs extra energy. These "interruptions" often come when we feel least able to respond.

These moments will test and reveal the relative strength of our commitments: Are we more committed to our own convenience or our relationships, to our work or our family, to our calendar or our church, to our checklist or our calling? Will we allow God to cancel our plans for the sake of others or cling to our established routines? Will we open our lives to the potential messiness and inconvenience of *koinōnia* relationships? As Dietrich Bonhoeffer reminds us, "We must be ready to allow ourselves to be interrupted by God. God will be constantly crossing our paths and canceling our plans by sending us people with claims and petitions."[2]

Though we seldom welcome interruptions, what if we shifted our perspective to see relational interruptions as divine opportunities God has placed before us? What if we lived attuned to the possibility that those inconveniences are instruments of God's transformative work, invitations to bless others, and, in God's upside-down ways, to find ourselves refreshed (Proverbs 11:25)? C. S. Lewis sums up this reality beautifully: "The great thing, if one can, is to stop regarding all the unpleasant things as interruptions of one's 'own,' or 'real' life. The truth is of course that what one calls the interruptions are precisely one's real life—the life God is sending one day by day."[3]

Covenantal Relationships

The promises of quick, easy, and hassle-free do not apply to human interactions, and approaching our relationships with a consumer mindset rather than a committed mindset leaves us and others utterly alone. Pastor Tim Keller defined a "consumer relationship" as one in which "the individual's needs are more important than the relationship." We hear subtle allusions to this consumer, "What's in it for me?" mentality in phrases like, "I tried, but it just didn't work" and "I wasn't getting anything out of it."

Keller contrasted consumer relationships with covenantal relationships, in which "the good of the relationship takes precedence over the immediate needs of the individual." Keller postulated the very idea of covenantal relationships is disappearing from our Western culture. "Sociologists argue that in contemporary Western society the marketplace has become so dominant that the consumer model increasingly characterizes most relationships that historically were covenantal."[4]

If our relationships are based on what's in it for me rather than mutual commitment to the other's good—whether consciously or not—those relationships will likely be short-lived. When our personal benefit ceases, the motivation for continuing the relationship will also cease.

Although this problem may be getting worse, it's nothing new. Early church father Isidore of Seville in the sixth century warned of the perils of this approach. Isidore said it this way:

> Those who are joined by benefit rather than grace are not faithful in friendship. For they will quickly desert unless they keep receiving benefit. An attachment created by benefit is dissolved when the benefit ceases.[5]

Keller expressed the same sentiment in more modern language:

> Today we stay connected to people only as long as they are meeting our needs at an acceptable cost to us. When we cease to make a profit—that is, when the relationship appears to require more love and affirmation from us than we are getting back—then we "cut our losses" and drop the relationship.[6]

We lack a foundation of commitment.

(Not Always) Happily Ever After

Most Americans were raised on fairy-tale endings, in which characters express some desire to commit to one another, then go on to live "happily-ever-after" lives. I (Phil) admit I'm a sucker for a happily-ever-after ending and have embarrassed myself more than once by blubbering in a theater or on an airplane.

I watched the movie *Lion* for the first time on a flight home from Africa. The flight attendant arrived to take my drink order just as the main character was reunited with his long-lost mother. "Diet Coke, please," I blubbered, tears flowing freely.

"What are you watching?" she asked kindly as she poured my drink.

"*Lion*," I responded, surreptitiously wiping away my tears.

"Thought so," she replied, with a knowing, sympathetic smile. I suspect I wasn't the first blubbering, *Lion*-watching passenger she had served.

We all love and long for the satisfaction of a happily-ever-after ending. Outside the realm of fairy tales, however, this expectation can be an impediment to the relationships we're meant to have. It idealizes and glosses over the work of commitment, leaving us saying, "This isn't what I signed up for!" when we face sacrifice, inconvenience, or conflict.

Though our culture celebrates the value of grit as a determiner of success and achievement in the marketplace, the same principle doesn't seem to be applied to our relationships. For most of us, it doesn't take long to think of a relationship that went south: where offense won out, busyness choked out time for one another, or one party's neediness became too much for the other. Cutting ties may or may not feel painful in the moment, but it more deeply entrenches our aloneness over time. Could it be that our vision of "happily ever after" excuses a lack of relational tenacity?

In looking for our happily ever after (not just romantically but in any relationship or community), we might end up with an epidemic of loneliness. As Dietrich Bonhoeffer warned in *Life Together*, "He who loves his dream of a community more than Christian community itself becomes a destroyer of the latter."[7] Unrealistic expectations for our relationships can sabotage actual community. Communities—comprised of flawed people—will face challenges, differences, and disagreements. We will love one another imperfectly. But we can't abandon the effort. We must remain committed.

A Rwandan proverb conveys a similar sentiment: "If you are building a house and the nail breaks, do you stop building the house?" Too often we do—leaving friends, spouses, and churches for greener pastures. A realistic view of the journey acknowledges the likelihood of ups and downs, highs and lows, and times of great challenge as well as joy.

While we certainly don't mean to imply there will never be a time when it may be necessary to cut ties, we take issue with severing bonds as a default response to every relational turmoil or dissatisfaction. In building a relational house, nails *will* break, but that's no reason to abandon building the house. Imagine walking through a neighborhood in which the streets were lined with unfinished houses. It would feel odd—even eerie. Abandoned relationships, like unfinished houses, should disturb and unsettle us.

Our friend Renee shared a story that resonated deeply with us. In her mid-twenties, Renee was part of a close group of friends. They were all single women pursuing careers, and they did life together, meeting weekly for Bible or book studies and connecting regularly in between to share about their joys, struggles, and daily lives. Their closeness grew over a few years as they invested time and effort in their relationships.

Then one friend, Kristine, began to wrestle with her faith. Over time, she recognized her beliefs no longer aligned with what her friends believed, and she decided to part ways with the group. This relational rupture was painful for all involved. None of the women wanted to sever their bond with Kristine. And so Renee determined that she wouldn't.

Although Renee couldn't force Kristine to reclaim her faith or reconsider her decision to cut ties with the group, she wanted her friend to know that her commitment remained, regardless. "Kristine," Renee said, "you can leave the group. That's your choice. But I'm not leaving you. You are too special to me, and I deeply value our friendship." To this day, Renee continues "building the house" of their relationship, calling Kristine regularly to check in and continuing to spend time together.

Committed relationships are not fairy-tale endings; in reality, commitment is more like a beginning than an ending. Without a foundational commitment, none of us can feel truly safe in our relationships, so they will remain surface level. We will feel tacit pressure to perform in certain ways or present a polished façade. We may not be honest about who we are and how we feel. We certainly won't want to risk being perceived—because of choice or circumstance—as needy, dependent, or uninteresting, so we'll keep our struggles to ourselves. In short, it will be difficult to know one another as we described in chapter four without commitment. The one-anothers are mutually reinforcing.

Without commitment we cannot experience the relationships we long for and the interdependent life God designed. As we learned from our brothers and sisters around the world, joy, peace, and a sense of rightness flow out of commitment, being there for one another. If we're asking, "What's in it for me?" then we're asking the wrong question. Let's try this instead: How do we love one another in the way of our committed King?

A Committed King

Jesus was all about relationships. With his limited time on earth, he lived, day in, day out, with a motley crew of disciples who regularly seemed to misunderstand his ways. As ambassadors of an upside-down kingdom, the disciples often fell short, yet Jesus remained committed to them and to the work of relationships. We get perhaps the clearest glimpse into how Jesus modeled relational commitment in his relationship with his disciple and dear friend Peter.

Peter was a handful, to say the least. Highs and lows, brash, impulsive, speaking before thinking. He was the first disciple to confess Jesus as the Messiah and the only one to dare walking on water, but he also cut off the ear of the high priest's servant though Jesus preached turning the other cheek, rebuked Jesus for foretelling his own death, rebuffed Jesus' offer to wash his feet, and slumbered when Jesus pleaded with him to pray. As they walked together closely, there were almost certainly more tensions, blunders, slips of the tongue, and rough edges not recorded for posterity.

But one instance recorded in every Gospel had to be the most heartbreaking failure of them all: Peter denied Jesus in his time of greatest need. Matthew, Mark, and Luke say that Peter "wept bitterly" or "broke down and wept" afterward (Matthew 26; Mark 14; Luke 22). He hadn't turned Jesus over to the authorities as Judas had, but as Jesus turned to look at him (Luke 22:61), Peter must have realized that he, too, had betrayed his friend.

After Jesus' crucifixion, Peter was out at sea one morning, fishing with some of the other disciples, when he saw Jesus standing on the shore (John 21). Recalling his denials, Peter might have both longed for and dreaded a reunion with Jesus. But true to his impulsive form, he leaped out of the boat and into the water, swimming to reach Jesus as quickly as possible.

Peter's track record as a disciple and friend was spotty, and he knew it. But Jesus didn't reprimand Peter, give him the cold shoulder, demand an apology, or calmly explain that they would have to cut ties now because Peter had fallen short one too many times. Instead, Jesus had an amazing, reconciling conversation with Peter: *Do you love me? Then feed my sheep.* Jesus communicated his ongoing commitment to Peter by inviting Peter to renew *his* commitment—both to him as a disciple and to the church. *Are you still with me? Because I'm still with you.*

In our culture, many would have advised Jesus to cut ties with Peter. (We confess we would have had some qualms with this friendship!) Jesus had every justification to move on or communicate a firm boundary, but instead he built a bridge. He was not "done" with Peter or replacing him with a more faithful, less error-prone follower. He didn't disavow this member of his community who had disowned him or say, "I care about you, but come back to me when you've worked things out."

Jesus' commitment to their relationship was unwavering: *I'm not giving up on you.* This was covenantal love: the kind Jesus spoke of when he told the disciples, "I've laid down a pattern for you" (John 13:14-15 MSG), and "This is how everyone will recognize that you are my disciples—when they see the love you have for each other" (John 13:35 MSG). Jesus' teachings are quite clear. He never said, "Serve others so they will serve you." He said to serve others in the same sacrificial posture he modeled (Matthew 20:28). He never said, "Love others as they love you." He said to love one another "as I have loved you" (John 13:34).

In every sustained relationship, we will move between seasons of reciprocity and seasons of unequal investment, times of "one another" and "do unto others." Though *allēlōn* invites mutual commitment, we will be misled if we equate "mutual" with "win-win": a subtle variation on "WIIFM," still focused on me. Christlike covenantal love demands relational tenacity.

"All In" to ALL In

In my early thirties, I (Phil) received an unexpected opportunity to demonstrate committed, covenantal love to my dear friend Rick. Rick was one of those guys who let his light shine brightly. We worked together, worshiped together, and even lived in the same neighborhood, so I saw a lot of Rick, and I was greatly blessed by our encouraging, safe, and transparent friendship. For a season, our relationship might have looked like the picture-perfect example of *allēlōn*: Everything about it was mutual and mutually satisfying.

Rick loved being a dad to his five-year-old son and was overjoyed to learn that his wife was expecting twins. He couldn't wait to welcome two new lives to their growing family. But the joy of that announcement was soon overshadowed by devastating news: Rick had fast-moving, evasive cancer. There was a lot to do in balancing cancer treatments and prenatal preparations, but my wife Becca and I were committed to bearing this burden with our friends. We were "all in," helping Rick and his wife prepare for the twins' arrival and navigate a new cancer diagnosis. Even so, Rick's condition deteriorated rapidly.

Rick needed a liver transplant, and miraculously his medical team secured a match. But just months after receiving the new liver, Rick's body rejected the organ, and he passed away. Suddenly his wife was shouldering the load of settling Rick's affairs, caring for infant twins, continuing to pour into their five-year-old, and finding a job to support the family. This was no longer a temporary storm but an ongoing reality of life without Rick. There was no quick fix for a life event of this magnitude.

For Becca and me, as close and committed friends, being "all in" rapidly escalated to being all-consumed. The elevated and sustained level of need Rick's family was experiencing entirely overwhelmed our emotional and physical resources. The season stretched us immensely as we walked with the family through the grieving process as well as the practicalities of moving forward. While I'd love to report that I was the model of *ezer*, the joyful servant always ready to run to the rescue, I'll confess there were times I joined the psalmist in asking, "How long, O LORD?" To be honest, this commitment soon became most of the things we fear commitment will be: costly, inconvenient, time-consuming, and draining.

Though we remained committed, Becca and I made a mistake that we only identified in retrospect. Whether out of pride or self-imposed expectations, we held on to a streak of independent self-sufficiency—*we've got this ("all in")*—that actually sidelined the power of *koinōnia* commitment *(ALL of us in)*. *Koinōnia* was a very real part of our church community at the time, probably more than we've ever experienced elsewhere. There were many others who, at a moment's notice, would have joyfully come alongside us to serve if we'd made space for them to do so. While our commitment was deep, we fell prey to an equal depth of independence, going it alone and forsaking the opportunity for our community to be all in this together.

Our independent commitment didn't serve us well as we swiftly approached burnout, nor did it serve Rick's family well to be so reliant on us alone. When a work transfer moved us to another city, they were once again left scrambling for support. It never would have happened if the load were shared by a committed *koinōnia* community rather than shouldered singlehandedly. Our go-it-alone approach was contrary to God's intent. Another African saying comes to mind: "If you want to go fast, go alone; if you want to go far, go together." As we walked alongside Rick's family, I learned a lot about enduring commitment—a large part of which is sustained in the power of *koinōnia*. Embracing our interdependence is core to embracing commitment, and once again, savings group members showed us the *koinōnia* way.

God's Intent for Community

Over the years, we've seen countless savings group members around the world embrace commitment not begrudgingly but eagerly. As we noted earlier, they seem to see commitment as a joy rather than a burden. And because commitment rarely conjures that same feeling in us, we were eager to understand more about what mindsets and practices facilitated that perspective.

Several years ago, HOPE International's team in Rwanda shared the story of a savings group member named Jeanette whose life had been transformed by one of the clearest manifestations of *koinōnia* that we've ever seen. Jeanette grew up rejected by a physically and verbally abusive stepfather. One day, he drove her from the family's home, knowing she had nowhere else to turn.

Jeanette hadn't yet finished school, and her body had been weakened by her stepfather's repeated beatings, so she had little in the way of marketable skills. She met her daily needs by begging and lived under an old mosquito net among some bushes just outside town. Jeanette's living conditions left her vulnerable to the elements, illness, and further abuse. She became pregnant through rape, and soon there were two living under a tattered mosquito net among the shrubbery.

The stigma of unwed motherhood is very strong in many countries, and Rwanda is no exception. The church Jeanette had long attended excommunicated her when they learned she was pregnant. Tending to the needs of a baby as well as herself only added to the practical challenges Jeanette faced, but Jeanette, who was deeply isolated, considered her son a blessing as a source of love and companionship.

Soon Jeanette met a female pastor who assured her she would be welcomed among her congregation. Jeanette began attending church, and the pastor connected her with a small group, which happened to be one of the HOPE-sponsored savings groups that met to pool their resources as well as study the Bible and fellowship.

For existing members of the savings group, there was every reason to back away or close ranks. This was one needy person: no job, no spouse, no family support, and a young son. Add to that the societal scourge Jeanette carried, even being thrown out of her former church. It all added up to *messy*. The group was doing fine without the interruption. They might have responded, "We've got enough to worry about just taking care of our families and each other. Our plates are sufficiently full." But instead, they committed to Jeanette.

The group members had little money, but Jeanette had least of all. In the beginning, they saved just pennies a week, yet those small savings were more than Jeanette could muster. Wanting to contribute fully to the group, Jeanette began a water delivery service, carrying water in jerry cans from a public tank to neighbors' homes for a small fee so she could save some of her earnings.

The group met together week after week, and their bonds continued to deepen. Over time, they became aware of Jeanette and her son's living conditions. One day, the group's president could take it no longer. "How can we continue to sleep in our beautiful houses and keep changing clothes for our spouses and children while our daughter Jeanette sleeps in the bush with no food or clothes and no tent to cover her baby boy during the sunny or rainy season? It is a shame before God and his people."

Tears flowed freely as group members unanimously expressed their resolve to use what little they had to build a house for Jeanette, committing both their resources and time. At the very next meeting, they came with hoes, machetes, and axes, clearing land to build the home's foundation. In the weeks to come, they shaped bricks and built walls. They volunteered their time, used the group's emergency fund to purchase supplies, and gave from their personal funds as well. The community couldn't help but notice. Some mocked their efforts, but others were moved.

One older group member remembers how neighbors told her she was too old to exert herself in this effort. They said she was crazy, but she could not be dissuaded. "Though I could not carry a big jerry can or contribute extra money, I wanted to help her. I wanted to use my hands and energy." She continued, "We showed our neighbors that a church is not just a temple but a loving and caring family."

Jeanette was overcome by the group's generosity. When she and her son moved into the house, she dedicated it as a house of prayer. Every Friday night, she opened her home for prayer meetings, and according to her pastor, ten community members became believers as a result.

Koinōnia Commitment

It is a beautiful story of *koinōnia*, and we long for it to end here, where God has clearly moved to bring beauty from ashes (happily ever after). Sadly, though Jeanette's estranged family had permitted the group to build the home on a far-flung corner of their property, they later recanted and laid claim to the house. Jeanette decided to start fresh in another town, safe from the abuse of her estranged family but also removed from proximity to her savings group, which had become her true family. When we spoke with group members about this messy, unresolved ending, we wondered if their efforts and investment, their commitment to Jeanette, felt wasted. In hindsight, would they do it again? The question almost didn't compute. Of course they would do it again: Jeanette is family.

This is *koinōnia*.

We are struck by how this story diverges from most in our experience. First, this group saw and spoke of Jeanette as family. It wasn't just that the group opposed homelessness in the aggregate. In addressing Jeanette's homelessness, they saw themselves building a home for their daughter or sister. They committed to her as a member of their family. Kingdom relationships break the boundaries of earthly kinship.

Second, they recognized the sufficiency of what they had. A consumer mindset would have had this group focusing on using their savings to acquire more or finer clothes or build larger, fancier houses. By our standards what they had was barely sufficient, but the group's president described "beautiful houses" and changes of clothes as though they were abundant. How often we've eschewed commitment because of perceived scarcity—whether time, abilities, or money.

Next, it was not just one or two in the group who were "all in;" the entire group was ALL in. *Every* group member committed to coming alongside Jeanette and their fellow group members in this endeavor. Any single member of the group who tried to tackle Jeanette's challenges in their own independent strength would have been overwhelmed, but they took a posture of interdependence—each relying on others, each lightening the load for someone else—and together they committed to Jeanette and her son.

I am "all in"　　　　　　　　　　**We are ALL in**

God invites us to be *ezers*, yes, but his design is for interdependent communities of commitment, not individual heroism. Without Spirit-born interdependence, commitment will not bring the joy these savings group members experienced. With it, every group member experienced the fulfillment of being on mission together and the reward of being a part of God's truly extraordinary work of placing the lonely in families (Psalm 68:6). So how can we do likewise?

Designing a Life of Commitment to One Another

This is our fifth and final one-another, and there's a reason we've saved it for last. Each one-another calls for transformation, whether subtle or significant: from independence to interdependence, hiddenness to openness, disengagement to dialogue, and exclusion to welcome. Each one leads us from heart change to relational change. And each requires more than good intentions—it calls for commitment.

The commitment we explore here is unique: It's relational. Unlike commitments to self-improvement—like healthy eating, exercise, or quiet time—this is an outward-facing commitment to others. We love one another by committing to each other: to serve, share, bear burdens, pray, rescue, and celebrate one another.

Even when we're convinced of its importance, commitment faces strong cultural headwinds: consumerism, convenience, and a "What's in it for me?" mentality. That's why the design suggestions in this section focus primarily on mindset and heart posture. Practicing commitment as God intended requires a new way of thinking about relationships. It may feel daunting—but God invites us to take one step at a time, however small.

Start with the heart. Begin by prayerfully assessing your relational mindset:

- Is my approach to relationships consumer-based or covenantal?

- How much does convenience shape my willingness to engage?

- When things get hard—when a "nail breaks"—do I keep building or walk away?

- Are my relationships marked by *ezer*, *allēlōn*, and *koinōnia*?

Let your answers to these questions guide your prayers and inform your next steps.

What can I do for you? Keep this question at the forefront of your mind. It reflects a posture of *ezer*—running to the rescue—and reinforces your commitment to others. Small acts matter: sitting with a grieving friend, offering a ride, or picking up a neighbor's mail.

Carry plenty of nails. Let go of the illusion of perfect community. Real relationships involve brokenness—and broken nails. Covenantal commitment comes with a pretty big bag of nails and requires our dedication to repair relational ruptures. Jesus went through plenty of nails with Peter—and with us. When adversity hits a relationship, lean in. Don't let conflict or unmet expectations cause you to walk away. Keep building the house.

Make the time. You might think, *I don't have time.* But time reflects priorities. Where do relationships and community fit in your life? Start small: a phone call, a walk, a coffee. Without intentionality, busyness will crowd out commitment. But you can choose to make time.

Sign up and stick with it. If your heart is ready but you're unsure where to begin, start by joining a group with a shared purpose. As we've observed in savings groups around the world, commitment grows in the soil of shared mission. Even if you don't know other group members yet, showing up consistently creates space for connection.

Take the long view. An African proverb says, "There are no shortcuts to the top of the palm tree." In a culture that values efficiency and convenience, we're trained to ask, "Is there an easier, less strenuous option?" But relationships take time. Research shows it can take over two hundred hours to build a close friendship.[8] There's no microwave version of community. Take the long view—and keep showing up.

Assess bandwidth and boundaries. We all have limits. As Rev. Joel Eidsness astutely observed, even Jesus had circles of closeness—120 followers, seventy followers, twelve disciples, three close friends, and one most intimate friend.[9] Boundaries are necessary, but a boundary that says, "If it requires effort, I'm out," or "Hurt my feelings and I'm out" is less a boundary than a barrier to the relationships God intended. As author and speaker Jennie Allen reminds us, "We've gotten so good at boundaries that we've forgotten how to forgive and love."[10] Where have you drawn lines that may need to be redrawn?

ALL-in **koinōnia** *community.* Do you have an ALL-in *koinōnia* community? If not, ask God to help you find one. If you're in a group but not experiencing *ezer, allēlōn,* and *koinōnia,* be the spark. Model these postures within your group. Share these ideas (and accompanying resources available at waybacktooneanother.com) with your group. Our most transformative experiences have come in communities marked by deep, mutual commitment. We've seen this in savings groups—where people care for each other through crises, help one another farm fields, and pay school fees for orphans. Their commitment runs deep. And when everyone is ALL in, the impact multiplies.

We Are ALL In

Becca and I (Phil) live in Lancaster, Pennsylvania. While Lancaster is known for its large Amish population, over the years it has also been known for warmly welcoming refugees, ranking as one of the top few counties in the United States for refugee resettlement per capita. Our church is committed to serving the local community, including our newest neighbors.

Several months ago, Becca and I joined a group from our congregation in welcoming and supporting a refugee family of nine: a mother, father, and their seven beautiful children, ages six to twenty. Refugee resettlement is a lot: There are mandatory medical, dental, and vision exams along with follow-ups, vaccinations, language classes, school registrations, and applications for various services. We've multiplied many of these steps by nine, as each family member must navigate the process. The parents and older siblings must additionally shop for groceries, learn to pay bills, open bank accounts, meet with schoolteachers, secure work permits, search for jobs, apply for driver's licenses, and more.

It's a daunting, overwhelming list for any would-be helper to contemplate. But our team of twelve has not been overwhelmed. Some team members bring unique expertise in a particular area, like medical, education, social work, or business. Their technical expertise is a blessing and put to use so effectively! But an attribute that wouldn't show up on any résumé is the deep commitment we each bring to the task and to each other.

A shared calendar and WhatsApp chat help us track the myriad appointments, events, and meetings, indicating which team member has volunteered to help. And volunteer we do, each of us to the extent we are able. We're *ALL in*. We all have jobs and families, and we regularly encourage one another to maintain a healthy balance. Comments like these are the norm: "Jan, let me take that; your plate is full right now," or "John, I'm free if you want me to handle that. I've seen your name on the calendar a lot lately." We're committed to caring for each other, just as we're committed to caring for our new neighbors.

Interruptions, unanticipated and sometimes inconvenient, are a regular occurrence. "My daughter has a fever. Could anyone take my place driving to English classes?" "The school just scheduled a meeting with the counselor this afternoon. Can someone be there?" "I just got a call that their car won't start. Could someone run by the house to help out?" "Their son is in the emergency room. Could someone wait with them until he can be seen?" Almost always, within a minute or two of the "cry for help," someone has jumped in to meet the need. There is an unspoken commitment to welcome interruptions! I continue to be inspired by my sisters and brothers whose commitment transcends convenience or personal comfort.

"What's in it for me?" doesn't seem to be a consideration in this *koinōnia* community, but the truth is our joy in this community has grown as our commitment has grown. While our goal may be to see our newly arrived neighbors resettled, we are reaping the benefits of deeper friendships and community that have resulted from commitment to each other on the journey. When we began, most of us didn't know each other well, and in some cases not at all. Today, we're far richer through the relationships we're experiencing. In many ways, I'd refer to these friends as my "welcome team" family. The joy of community continues to grow as we continue to commit. Christ-centered *koinōnia* community produces that.

Pursuing commitment over convenience, building bridges not just boundaries, and demonstrating tenacity in the face of relational challenges are countercultural preconditions for the life of togetherness Jesus invites us into. What a blessing that God is committed to us—and invites us to experience community as he intended when we commit to one another.

Reflect Individually

- Would you define your relationships as "consumer" or "covenantal"? What steps could you take to make your relationships more "covenantal"?

- How much of your time is committed to relationships? How does that compare with other ways you spend your time?

- How challenging is it for you to view the unplanned or unexpected needs of others as divine opportunities? How could you shift your mindset in that direction?

- If you aren't a part of a mutually committed community, what steps could you take to create it? What would you need to ask others to help you with?

Discuss Together

- Savings groups often describe themselves as a "family." How could we make our group more of a family?

- How committed are we to each other? How can we become willing to "drop everything" for one another?

- How does our group joyfully live out "ALL in" when we serve others?

- Jesus' relationship with Peter had many "broken nails," yet he kept "building the house." When is a relationship worth fighting for, and when is it time to let it go? How can you continue "building the house" in your relationships worth fighting for?

- What one or two steps will we take to move toward interdependent commitment?

TURNING BACK TO ONE ANOTHER

When Kyle and Alisa moved to Chicago, they had no family or friends nearby. Seeking discipleship and community, the couple joined a church small group, and over the last eight years, they've created something vastly richer than they anticipated. The relationships within their small group have grown into something Kyle struggles to put into words. "It's not even friendship anymore—it's family." His words echo those of the Rwandan matriarch.

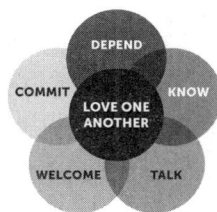

When we asked Kyle and Alisa to tell us more about their Chicago "family," we heard about Katie and Mario, peers who have become vacation buddies and confidants; Bretta and Oliver, a couple more than a decade their senior who shares their passion for community justice work; and Teresa and Nick, a retired couple whose wisdom has proven invaluable. The group's diversity in age, race, and background creates a rich blend of perspectives. Because we so often pursue relationships with people who closely resemble us (as the friendship study referenced in chapter six found), Kyle recognizes, "This group wouldn't be put together if you were deliberately assembling people. But that diversity has brought incredible wisdom to our relationships."

Like the savings groups we've highlighted throughout this book, Kyle's community of friends has cultivated meaningful practices that strengthen their relationships—practices that are neither obscure nor out of reach. Usually once a week they meet to share a meal. Much of their time together is the typical chatter of catching up, playing a game, laughing, watching a movie, just doing life together. These small, consistent choices have, over the years, built and sustained this community. Kyle said, "It's the boring and meaningless things that string together" to create something incredibly meaningful.

Their weekly check-ins have created space for vulnerability that's outside the norm in our independent culture. Consistency has contributed to transparency and a sense of being known. Their time together also includes some intentional design elements that aren't common to the average friendship. Whenever they gather, they set time aside for one person to share how they've seen God at work since they were last together—in everyday moments, nature, or art. These observations, which the group records in a journal, have taught each of them to notice what they might otherwise overlook, much like the practices we've seen in communities around the world. At the end of every year the team prepares dinner and Oliver prepares thoughtful questions to help the friends reflect together on the year's challenges and growth.

Kyle and Alisa knew from the start that belonging to this group helped them escape boredom and loneliness and feel connected in a new city. But when they walked through a journey of infertility, something far more significant became clear: Belonging to this group meant they were not alone.

"They have been there for every speed bump," Kyle shared, his voice softening. "It is comforting to know every week we had family who would cry with us, pray with us, show up for us when we've needed it. They know us so well that sometimes they don't need to say anything. I hope everyone has people in their lives where no words are needed; just their presence." Kyle and Alisa have experienced *ezer*, *allēlōn*, and *koinōnia* in action. They've been held by community, just as God intended.

They've also held others. Kyle shared that the group has walked through personal struggles, career transitions, and health scares with other members—all with the same unwavering support that he and Alisa experienced. When we asked what his life would look like without this community, Kyle found it almost impossible to imagine. "I can't picture life without them. I'd have a big relational hole," he said.

In a culture where independence is celebrated and busyness often gets in the way of meaningful connection, Kyle's community stands as a countercultural example of interdependence. They've moved from "me" to "we," embracing and applying the principles we've encouraged throughout this book: depending on, knowing, talking, welcoming, and committing to one another.

"It feels like we're part of a story together," Kyle said. Their story reminds us that authentic *koinōnia* community isn't built on grand gestures or programs but through simply showing up, over and over, with intentional care—rediscovering the way back to one another in joy and sorrow, the mundane and the memorable, the ordinary rhythms and the sacred moments.

Let's Turn the Ocean Liner

As author Malcolm Gladwell asserts in *The Tipping Point*, small, seemingly insignificant actions or changes can have outsized impacts.[1] Gladwell's conclusion echoes that of Naval lieutenant, systems theorist, and philosopher Buckminster Fuller. In 1972 when an interviewer asked Fuller his perspective on an individual's ability to "improve or even influence our own welfare, let alone that of society," Fuller responded with a metaphor. A massive ship, he said, is steered by a rudder. Even more subtly, it's steered by a tiny device on the rudder called a trim tab. With minimal effort, this small piece creates a pressure change that helps turn the whole ship.

Even when society seems to be moving in a different direction, Fuller asserted our small, thoughtful actions can influence the whole. Instead of trying to force change directly, by imposing programs or big-budget solutions akin to pushing back against the front of an ocean liner, we create and model subtle shifts that initiate real change, mimicking the understated methods of a trim tab.[2]

Until we engaged with savings groups around the world, we might not have believed that turning the tide on aloneness is possible. But after witnessing this transformation firsthand, we became convinced: We can catalyze not just enclaves but entire ecosystems of community through intentional design decisions.

We remain in pursuit of the way back to one another, even as we write. We haven't arrived at a point where we perfectly model the one-anothers, but we have become the test subjects of our own theory. To address our own longing for deeper, more meaningful relationships and community, we've engaged the trim tab in our own lives.

As we conclude, we want to share more on the steps we're taking. The specifics of how we've applied these insights to our lives look a bit different, and we imagine your journey will likewise be unique as you employ your own God-inspired solutions to the problem of aloneness.

Jeff's Reflections

I'm living differently than I was when Phil and I started this journey together. I've started facilitating classes for underemployed individuals seeking work and those learning to manage their finances. These sessions result in far more than just skill-building—we share meals, engage in genuine conversation, and meet outside of class to nurture friendships. I've made some great new friends in the process who are different from me in many ways but who make my life richer and lead me closer to Jesus.

I've turned away from the isolating noise of social media toward other connections—biking more with my wife, Christy, and building on shared interests in whitewater and downriver kayaking to create community with others. I also slow down to talk more. I've become more comfortable with schedule interruptions and opportunities for both casual chatter and extended, heartfelt, next-level conversations. Most importantly, I'm intentionally strengthening relationships, getting to know my next-door and across-the-street neighbors in ways I never prioritized before and expressing to my friends how much they truly mean to me—though this vulnerability still challenges me.

I'm also learning to simplify my life by saying no to more projects and obligations and creating greater margin for relationships in my schedule. As someone who naturally gravitates toward busyness and achievement, I've realized that having too many irons in the fire actually crowds out the relationships I value most. This intentional scaling back isn't easy for me—it goes against my instincts as an achiever—but I'm discovering that more margin creates more space for meaningful connections. When I'm not rushing from one obligation to the next, I have the bandwidth to notice when a neighbor needs help, to accept an impromptu invitation for coffee, or to just be present with those closest to me.

As I look ahead, perhaps the most exciting development is a group of friends I've convened—inspired by Kasie and Hannah and savings groups the world over—who are committed to lifelong friendship. I hope we will journey together for decades to come, meeting together regularly, pooling funds to give and even help each other out as needed, and always knowing we'll be each other's 3 a.m. friends.

Phil's Reflections

For a few years, Becca and I had been part of an amazing small group that truly leaned into *ezer*, *allēlōn*, and *koinōnia*. Just a few months ago, our group disbanded as several members entered a new season of life. There was no tension or dramatic breakup, and we've all stayed in contact individually—but I'm left with a relational ache, that "big relational hole" Kyle described.

We are praying for the next opportunity, knowing that God desires community for us still more than we desire it for ourselves. We're also actively embracing the postures we've seen catalyze community around the world, recognizing that we can co-create community—not just wait for it to find us. I'm prioritizing face-to-face interactions with those nearby or even voice-to-voice interactions with friends at a distance, and I've given up social media for this season of life. I've felt God's prompting: "You will never build community sitting comfortably by yourself on the couch."

It's not always comfortable, as initiating conversation doesn't come easily to me, but I'm pushing myself to be for others the person I longed to meet in seasons of aloneness. Conscious of the many times I've observed community within the church but felt excluded from it, I don't want that for others, so I'm intentional about spotting the person standing alone after church and introducing myself. Occasionally the "new" churchgoer, as it turns out, is only new to me, but even their gentle reply, "We've been attending for two years . . ." is an open door to conversation.

Before these interactions and others, I find myself repeating a simple prayer: "God, increase my sensitivity to those around me." It applies at home, at work, with neighbors, even on trips to the grocery store. I want to be attuned to the reality that we all need connection, many are lonely, and some I encounter today may need the compassion of a friendly greeting or a listening ear. In the checkout line, this might look like a warm and caring smile, followed by "How's your day?" With neighbors, it's often a gentle check-in like, "How's life been treating you?"

This past weekend, our neighbor was hosting a birthday party for his father. When I arrived, the guest of honor was sequestered upstairs at the kitchen table while attendees gathered and his family prepped downstairs. He sat alone sipping a beer, and as I entered he commented in jest that he'd been placed in the penalty box. His wife laughed and said to me, "Come on down!" But I knew exactly what I was going to do. "I'll just hang here with John," I replied. I sat down, smiled, and said, "Big day, huh? How ya doin'?"

It was clear John was in a reflective mood. Within a few minutes, he was reminiscing about his time in combat decades earlier. He choked back tears as he reflected on seeing friends and fellow soldiers gunned down. John and I aren't close friends, and I'd only known him as fun-loving and quick-witted. Yet, for whatever reason, the two of us alone at the kitchen table was safe space for him to open up. His wife soon called from downstairs that they were ready for the birthday boy.

He looked at me and said, "We'll talk more."

"I'd like that," I replied. We went downstairs, and I thanked God that he has answered my simple prayer for sensitivity over and over. Relational doors have been opened.

I'm also reminding myself to reframe interruptions as divine opportunities. A few weeks ago, I was enjoying what I felt was some well-deserved "me-time." As I sat on the couch riveted by the final round of the Masters golf tournament, my phone pinged with an incoming text message. It was a fellow church member, alerting me that our refugee friends' car wouldn't start and wondering if I might be available to help. Immediately, excuses swarmed in my mind, but I reminded myself this was a divine invitation. A couple hours later, our friends had a new car battery and a functioning vehicle. We shared high fives and a deepened bond of friendship. Looking back, I'm grateful to have accepted the invitation.

The Journey Begins

Through reflecting on the five one-anothers, we're learning to live them out more fully—discovering what Jesus modeled about mutual flourishing in his relationship with the Father and the Holy Spirit. The changes it's prompting are countercultural and counter-intuitively life-giving, as true discipleship most often is.

The way back to one another begins with a choice—a decision to live differently in a world that often pulls us apart. We invite you to join us in this transformation. Your decision to practice the five one-anothers in your daily life will ripple outward in ways you cannot yet imagine. Each act of genuine connection creates a current that, when joined with others, becomes powerful enough to move the ocean liner, changing the course of our isolated culture. The relationships we nurture today will become the community that sustains us and others down the road. Don't underestimate the impact of your willingness to depend on, fully know, talk with, welcome, and commit to each other.

In a world starved for connection, your choice to walk the path back to one another isn't just meaningful—it's revolutionary. Will you take this journey with us?

ACKNOWLEDGMENTS

From Phil and Jeff

Jill, you've partnered with us in writing, editing, and clarifying these ideas. Thanks for your patience as we've worked on this for such a long time! We seriously could not have done it without you.

Al Hsu and the entire InterVarsity Press team, what a gift and unexpected surprise it has been to partner with you on this project. It's truly an honor to be part of the IVP family!

We're grateful to and inspired by the pastors across the country who shared with us what aloneness looks like in your neighborhoods and how you're working to create community. Thank you for lending your input and insight to this project.

Rev. Joshua Nolt and Rev. Joel Eidsness, you shepherded us well in providing guidance on our biblical framework. Thank you!

Staff serving HOPE International and World Relief, you were so generous with your time, answering our questions about savings groups and cultural norms and sharing your insights with us. You are truly heroes on the frontlines in your dedication to the underserved.

Brian and the Chalmers Center team, we are beyond grateful for your visionary trailblazing of what we know today as Christ-centered and church-centered savings groups.

We're grateful to the many friends who shared their stories—and who've shared their lives—with us.

To Kyle, Sean, Rich, Ling, Douglas, Kaye, Jan, Kent, Steve, Claire, and Peter, thank you for providing feedback along the way. Your input helped tremendously to sharpen, clarify, and refine our message.

To Alyssa Reiff and Savannah Jeffery, your superb research skills and contributions shaped the ideas presented here. Iris Noth, your attention to detail and heart of service blessed us in the book's final stages.

Claire Brosius, LeAnna Vine, and Emily Lapian, we're grateful for your creativity and expert guidance as we've prepared to share this book with others.

To the HOPE International marketing team, particularly the creative writers, thank you for identifying and curating so many amazing stories of transformation, including those we've shared.

Underpinning all of these acknowledgments, we're so grateful to our heavenly Father for birthing the idea in us, orchestrating our collaboration, and guiding our journey. We are humbled and thankful.

"Now to him who is able to do immeasurably more than all we ask or imagine, according to his power that is at work within us, to him be glory in the church and in Christ Jesus throughout all generations, for ever and ever! Amen" (Ephesians 3:20-21).

From Jeff

Phil, I'm so grateful for the invitation to join you in writing this book. You are a treasured friend, and I look up to you for so many reasons. Now we can go back to just hanging out and goofing off without always talking about the book!

Kevin Ely, thank you for encouraging me to give writing a shot and helping me build the confidence that I can do it. Don't underestimate how much your encouragement has truly helped. Looking forward to another decade of lunches!

Pastor Craig, thank you for generously writing the foreword but even more so for modeling the values that lead to community throughout our church. I'm so proud to have you as my pastor!

Brian Fikkert, I'm grateful for your enduring friendship and theological influence, as well as your introductions that connected me and Life.Church to partners who have truly changed the trajectory of my life and directly led to this writing project.

Michelle, Kyle, Calla, Mark, Ron, Andrew, Ana, Paul, Talhia, Sadara, Aggrey, and the entire GLC crew, our story reflects so much of what Phil and I have written. You guys are the best! Together is the only way forward.

To Kayla, Austin, Linda, Krisa, Kyle, Talhia, Heather, Anna, and the entire Community Team at every Life.Church location—thank you not only for your encouragement along the way but also for your daily efforts to help people experience community. I truly love working with all of you.

Thank you to Laura, Rachel, Kellie, Jason, Abigail, Linda, and Hannah on the Life.Church team who've dedicated your time and skills to this project. Laura, because of your contributions, the questions posed in this book will prompt deeper reflection and more compelling conversation.

Jerry, few people are fortunate enough to work for a boss like you. I'm exceedingly grateful for your investment and influence in my life and your friendship over so many years. Thank you for your support of this project and your commitment to creating a culture of community throughout our team and church.

To new and old friends—you know who you are. Thank you for modeling the ideas in this book and for shaping me through our regular coffees, breakfasts, and lunches. You each mean so much to me. Here's to many more years together.

To my parents, Bob and Pat Galley, you've embodied the ideas represented in this book throughout your lifetime.

To my kids (and kids-in-law) Brenton and Tiffany, Ryan and Breanna, and Dustin and Jillian, your encouragement as I've worked on this project and your help in sharpening these ideas has been invaluable. I'm so proud of each of you. You are examples to me of what it means to seek community and care for others.

Christy, my wife of thirty-four years, thank you for your incredible support throughout this project and constant encouragement. I'm so grateful for our partnership in life and the gift of unconditional love and acceptance you've always given to me. You make me feel so comfortable to be myself. In the words of Drew Holcomb: "It's like puttin' on my favorite pair of shoes, I like to be with me, when I'm with you."[1] I love you!

From Phil

Jeff Galley, from the day we met about a decade ago, you have been a dear friend and encourager. Over time, you've become a brother. You inspire me! While you would humbly deny it, I see so much of the relational richness we've written about in your life. Thank you, brother!

Peter Greer, you've provided nonstop encouragement, counsel, cheerleading, and unwavering support through this entire journey. I'm so grateful. You've been there with us as one who has traveled this path before. Thank you. Now, as you say, "On we go!"

My best buddy Jeff Eberts passed away before this book came to print, but he modeled and taught me so much about listening and relational commitment. Thank you. I miss you. Sandy, his wife, who carries on the legacy of loving people: You're awesome.

Thank you, HOPE's leadership, for affording me the opportunity for this project, and to Dave, Chris, and Mark who walked with me in balancing priorities through the process. You guys have been great and supportive managers.

I'm grateful to so many colleagues at HOPE International, in our field operations and here in the United States, who have invested in me personally and spiritually, encouraged this book-writing journey, and remain committed to the amazing work to which HOPE is called.

To my family at Lancaster Brethren in Christ Church—pastors, home church, refugee welcome team, leadership team, and congregation—you exemplify in so many ways the community we've shared about in our writing.

To Emmanuel Ngoga, Erisa Mutabazi, and a multitude of brothers and sisters in Rwanda who taught me so much about culture and community, I'm so grateful for you!

To Sean, Su, Iranzi, Samantha, Oliver, and Diana—family! I'm proud to be your dad (and bobo), and I am so thankful for each of you! You're the best cheering-on team (and family) I could ever ask for. Your encouragement, thoughts, ideas, and feedback from the beginning have given wings to the journey!

Saving the best for last. Becca, you are amazing! I'm so grateful for your support through the highs and lows of the writing and rewriting, for your patience and encouragement. Added to that, you joined me in some transparent sharing about our journey. Thanks for being willing to risk being known. Our journey continues, and I'm so thankful for you. Love you a bunch!

ADDITIONAL RESOURCES

ADDITIONAL RESOURCES TO SUPPLEMENT this book are available at *waybacktooneanother.com*. These include a discussion guide, a recommended reading list, and a self-assessment tool designed to help you explore your own level of "one-another" engagement. You'll find tools to foster both personal reflection and group discussion on the way back to one another.

ONE-ANOTHER VERSES

THE GREEK WORD ALLĒLŌN, translated "one another," is found over one hundred times in the New Testament. Of these, forty-seven are direct instructions to Christ-followers from Jesus, Peter, John, James, and Paul (with 60 percent coming from Paul).

Love

1. Love one another. (John 13:34; 15:12, 17; Romans 13:8; 1 Thessalonians 3:12; 4:9; 1 Peter 1:22; 1 John 3:11; 4:7, 11; 2 John 5)

2. Be devoted to one another in love. (Romans 12:10)

3. Tolerate one another in love. (Ephesians 4:2)

Unity

1. Be at peace with one another. (Mark 9:50)

2. Don't grumble among one another. (John 6:43)

3. Be of the same mind with one another. (Romans 12:16; 15:5-6)

4. Wait for one another before beginning the Eucharist. (1 Corinthians 11:33)

5. Don't bite, devour, and consume one another. (Galatians 5:15)

6. Don't boastfully challenge or envy one another. (Galatians 5:26)

7. Don't complain against one another. (James 4:11; 5:9)

8. Maintain marital unity. (1 Corinthians 7:5)

Humility

1. Give preference to one another in honor. (Romans 12:10)

2. Regard one another as more important than yourselves. (Philippians 2:3)

3. Don't be haughty: Be of the same mind. (Romans 12:16)

4. Be subject to one another. (Ephesians 5:21)

5. Seek good for one another, and don't repay evil for evil. (1 Thessalonians 5:15)

6. Clothe yourselves in humility toward one another. (1 Peter 5:5)

Openness and Transparency

1. Accept one another. (Romans 15:7)

2. Confess sins to one another. (James 5:16)

3. Speak truth to one another. (Ephesians 4:25)

4. Don't lie to one another. (Colossians 3:9)

5. Do not judge one another, and don't put a stumbling block in another's way. (Romans 14:13)

6. Bear with and forgive one another. (Colossians 3:13)

7. Gently, patiently tolerate one another. (Ephesians 4:2)

8. Be kind, tenderhearted, and forgiving to one another. (Ephesians 4:32 NKJV)

Encouragement

1. Bear one another's burdens. (Galatians 6:2)

2. Comfort one another concerning the resurrection. (1 Thessalonians 4:13-18)

3. Pray for one another. (James 5:16)

4. Encourage and build up one another. (1 Thessalonians 5:11)

5. Stimulate one another to love and good deeds. (Hebrews 10:24)

Service and Hospitality

1. Serve one another (Galatians 5:13)

2. Wash one another's feet. (John 13:14)

3. Show hospitality to one another without grumbling. (1 Peter 4:9)

4. Welcome one another. (Romans 15:7)

5. Greet one another with a kiss. (Romans 16:16; 1 Corinthians 16:20; 2 Corinthians 13:12; 1 Peter 5:14)

A NOTE TO CHURCH LEADERS

As a pastor, I (Jeff) want nothing more than for each person God has brought to our church to experience everything he intends for them. Jesus said he came to give us the fullest life (John 10:10), and I long to see everyone living this abundant life that's on offer. I also know that's often not the case, because this kind of life isn't possible without strong, interdependent relationships so many lack. God designed us for these connections, and Jesus said the world would recognize us as his followers by the way we love. Our relationships are meant to help us and others encounter Jesus more deeply.

But research shows disconnection from others is often as prevalent among churchgoers as among our broader society. If we've been called to lives of love and connection, why isn't the church in the United States doing more to fight loneliness? From personal observation, I'd say that many, if not most, churches *are* trying, but our predominant approach isn't working as well as we'd hope. Many church leaders try to fix the problem of aloneness through programs. We use small groups, care teams, greeters, and other ways to make people feel welcomed and connected. While these efforts are valuable, they fall short of addressing the root issue because the solution we need is not primarily programmatic; it's cultural.

Church culture is far more powerful than a program. Programs are limited and focused on a specific task. They work within set parameters and often have short lifespans. By contrast, culture comprises the deep beliefs, values, and actions that shape how people within our congregations think, act, and make decisions. Culture affects every part of a church's life and leaves a lasting mark in a way that no program can.

There's nothing wrong with programs; we need small groups and the structures that support them. We need leaders who give their time and effort to make others feel loved, known, and welcomed. I'm not suggesting we stop these initiatives. What I am suggesting is that we don't expect more from these programs than they can deliver. We need to cultivate an accompanying culture of interdependence, authenticity, and commitment to one another. To create churches where *koinōnia* thrives, we must focus on forming a different culture.

Culture is shaped by three key elements:

- Values: What do we prioritize and celebrate as a church?

- Norms: What unspoken rules guide how we interact and care for one another?

- Language: What words and stories do we use to reinforce a sense of belonging?

By intentionally shaping these elements, we can create a culture that naturally and powerfully combats aloneness and fosters the kind of meaningful connections we all desire. Unfortunately, shaping culture is far easier said than done.

As leaders in the church, this begins with our own lives. People are more influenced by how they see us living than by what we say. We tend to reproduce who we are, not just what we advocate. The apostle Paul understood this, as he encouraged the church to follow his example as he followed the example of Christ (1 Corinthians 11:1).

In the "Design a Life" section of each chapter in this book, we've offered suggestions that anyone can live out to embody the one-another commands we've explored. That's where all of us, including leaders, need to start if we intend to create and maintain church cultures that eradicate aloneness. We have to model this abnormal, countercultural way of living in our own lives. Christianity is at its best when it is countercultural, so as leaders we must live in a countercultural way if we have any hope that others will follow. Some of the pastors we interviewed shared inspiring examples.

Heather and her husband, Josh, lead a suburban church in the Dallas/Fort Worth area. Recognizing isolation as pervasive in their suburb, they've shifted their church services to place community front and center by transitioning from rows of seating to circular tables with "hosts," discussion guides, and sharing time built into their Sunday morning service. But Pastor Heather is quick to note that she seeks to practice authenticity and inclusivity in her own life and to share about it vocally, which in turn shapes the culture of the church.

In St. Louis, Missouri, Will pastors a church in a community beset by isolation, economic challenges, and racial tensions. He is strategically, consciously designing an environment where people can embrace their imperfections and find true belonging—an enclave set apart from much of the isolation and tension affecting the broader community—by going first in practicing vulnerability, sharing his own flaws from the pulpit.

To shape a culture of caring and belonging, we'll need to talk about it—often. Share stories from your own life, including those that reflect your imperfect attempts at loving others in the way of Jesus. Normalize both the importance and the difficulty of the one-anothers. Highlight stories of those within your congregation who are modeling these values. When we live out these principles, talk about them regularly, and share stories often, they begin to feel natural—becoming our default posture. The more we engage in this shared language, the more it reinforces the culture we're trying to build.

As young adults, Justin, the founding pastor of a church in New England, and nine of his friends bought houses next to each other, living and worshiping together. They established a church and have had the privilege of watching God multiply its attendance since those early days. But as the friends married and began families, life started to pull them in different directions. In recent years they realized they'd drifted from their core value of genuine community. It was no longer the norm, even among their staff. Justin publicly acknowledged his own drift in this core commitment, and he's found that as he's reconnecting with that value and once again seeking vibrant community, sharing his personal journey is helping many more in his church body turn the tide against aloneness in their own lives. He shares his priorities, which include spending time with others, practicing vulnerability, giving to benefit others, not taking himself too seriously, and taking following Jesus very seriously.

At Life.Church I benefit from a culture of community that began long before I joined the team nearly two decades ago. Even in my interview (detailed in chapter four) I benefited from the team's transparency, support, and commitment to Christ-centered community. We are very far from perfect, and we readily admit that we don't always do what we've written in this book. But I'm grateful that early on, Life.Church's founding pastor Craig Groeschel lived out the values of being authentically known and committed to one another. He's been modeling these principles for three decades, and week after week I see the payoff.

If this is not the current culture of your church, know that shifting culture takes time. Don't expect immediate results.

Continue to pray and to model the culture you hope to see replicated. God will bring change, because even more than we desire to see aloneness eradicated and the lonely placed in families, *he* desires those things. He wants our churches to be places where people care and belong even more than we want that for our churches. He wants to reshape our church cultures, and he's looking for partners.

NOTES

Introduction: Longing for Something More

[1]"Measuring Poverty," World Bank Group, last updated June 5, 2025, www
.worldbank.org/en/topic/measuringpoverty.

1. Eyes Open to a Better Way

[1]Johann Hari, *Chasing the Scream: The First and Last Days of the War on Drugs*
(Bloomsbury, 2016), 293.

[2]Jessica Buechler, "The Loneliness Epidemic Persists: A Post-Pandemic Look at
the State of Loneliness Among U.S. Adults," The Cigna Group Newsroom, accessed September 12, 2025, https://newsroom.thecignagroup.com/all-stories
?item=446.

[3]Vivek Murthy, *Our Epidemic of Loneliness and Isolation: The U.S. Surgeon General's Advisory on the Healing Effects of Social Connection and Community* (US
Public Health Service, 2023), 8, www.hhs.gov/sites/default/files/surgeon-general
-social-connection-advisory.pdf.

[4]Ellyn Maese, "Almost a Quarter of the World Feels Lonely," *Gallup*, October 24,
2023, https://news.gallup.com/opinion/gallup/512618/almost-quarter-world
-feels-lonely.aspx.

[5]Daniel A. Cox, "The State of American Friendship: Change, Challenges, and Loss,"
The Survey Center on American Life, June 8, 2021, www.americansurveycenter.org
/research/the-state-of-american-friendship-change-challenges-and-loss/.

[6]Barna, "What We've Learned About Relational Flourishing," *Barna Group*,
April 1, 2020, https://barna.gloo.us/articles/relational-flourishing-learnings.

[7]Department for Digital, Culture, Media & Sport, "Joint Message from the UK and
Japanese Loneliness Ministers," GOV.UK, June 17, 2021, www.gov.uk/government
/news/joint-message-from-the-uk-and-japanese-loneliness-ministers.

[8]Barna, *The Connected Generation* (Barna Group, 2019).

[9]Cigna, *Loneliness in America 2025: A Pervasive Struggle Requires a Communal
Response* (The Cigna Group, 2025), 7, https://filecache.mediaroom.com/mr5mr
_thecignagroup/183661/2025-loneliness-in-america-report-the-cigna-group.pdf.

[10]Barna, *Connected Generation,* 12.

[11]Harvard Kennedy School, *Harvard Youth Poll* 50 (Harvard Kennedy School Institute of Politics, 2025), https://iop.harvard.edu/youth-poll/50th-edition -spring-2025.

[12]Harvard Medicine, "The Good Life: An Interview with Robert Waldinger," *The Magazine of Harvard Medical School* (Fall 2022), https://magazine.hms.harvard .edu/articles/good-life.

[13]Robert D. Putnam, "Bowling Alone: America's Declining Social Capital," *Journal of Democracy* 6, no. 1 (1995): 65-78, https://dx.doi.org/10.1353/jod.1995.0002.

[14]Murthy, *Our Epidemic of Loneliness and Isolation,* 4.

[15]Julianne Holt-Lunstad et al., "Advancing Social Connection as a Public Health Priority in the United States," *American Psychological Association* 72, no. 6 (2017): 517-30, in Vivek Murthy, *Our Epidemic of Loneliness and Isolation: The U.S. Surgeon General's Advisory on the Healing Effects of Social Connection and Community,* (US Public Health Service, 2023), 8.

[16]"Loneliness Can Lead to Increased Risk of Heart Disease and Stroke," *University of York,* April 20, 2016, www.york.ac.uk/news-and-events/news/2016/research /loneliness-stroke-heart/.

[17]"Suicide Data and Statistics," Centers for Disease Control and Prevention, Suicide Prevention, March 26, 2025, www.cdc.gov/suicide/facts/data.html#cdc _data_surveillance_section_4-suicide-rates.

[18]The rate of those who currently have or are being treated for depression has risen from 10.5 percent in 2015 to 17.8 percent in 2023. Dan Witters, "U.S. Depression Rates Reach New Highs," *Gallup,* May 17, 2023, https://news.gallup.com/poll /505745/depression-rates-reach-new-highs.aspx.

[19]See broadly accepted definitions of these terms at "Social Connection," World Health Organization, June 30, 2025, www.who.int/news-room/questions-and -answers/item/social-connection.

[20]Susan Mettes, *The Loneliness Epidemic* (Brazos Press, 2021), 89.

[21]Barna, *The Connected Generation* (Barna Group, 2019), 28.

[22]Barna, "7-Year Trends: Pastors Feel More Loneliness and Less Support," *Barna Group,* July 12, 2023, www.barna.com/research/pastor-support-systems/.

[23]Mettes, *Loneliness Epidemic,* 106.

[24]Russell Moore, "Why the American Church Can't Fix Loneliness," *Christianity Today,* August 14, 2024, www.christianitytoday.com/2024/08/american-church -loneliness-russell-moore-social-capital-put/.

[25]Stephen Blandino, personal interview with Jeff Galley, December 16, 2021.

26Ryan Egli, personal communication with the authors, January 26, 2022.

27Wayne Watson, "Friend of a Wounded Heart," music by Wayne Watson, lyrics by Wayne Watson and Claire Cloninger, recorded 1987, track 4 on *Watercolor Ponies,* ASCAP, used by permission.

28Rodney Stark, *The Triumph of Christianity: How the Jesus Movement Became the World's Largest Religion* (HarperOne, 2011), 116-17.

2. It's as Simple and as Hard as That

1Dietrich Bonhoeffer, *Life Together,* trans. John W. Doberstein (Harper Collins, 1954), 111.

2For more on the Trinity, we recommend: (1) Michael Reeves, *Delighting in the Trinity: An Introduction to the Christian Faith* (IVP Academic, 2012) and (2) Tara-Leigh Cobble, *The Joy of the Trinity: One God, Three Persons* (B&H Books, 2024).

3Irwyn L. Ince Jr., *The Beautiful Community: Unity, Diversity, and the Church at Its Best* (InterVarsity Press, 2020), 54.

4Strong's Hebrew Lexicon (ESV), s.v. "H5828—'ēzer," in Blue Letter Bible, accessed June 18, 2025, www.blueletterbible.org/lexicon/h5828/esv/wlc/0-1/.

5Oxford University Press, in Oxford Languages via Google Dictionary, s.v. "succor," accessed September 12, 2025; "Succour," Bible Hub, accessed September 12, 2025, https://biblehub.com/topical/s/succour.htm.

6Jeffrey Kranz, "All the 'One Another' Bible Verses in One Infographic," Overview-Bible, March 9, 2014, https://overviewbible.com/one-another-infographic/.

7Eberhard Arnold, "Life's Task," (Bruderhof Historical Archive, 2019), www.eberhardarnold.com/explore/all-articles/2019/12/12/lifes-task.

3. Depend on One Another

1Patrick van Kessel and Laura Silver, "Where Americans Find Meaning in Life Has Changed over the Past Four Years," Pew Research Center, November 18, 2021, www.pewresearch.org/short-reads/2021/11/18/where-americans-find-meaning-in-life-has-changed-over-the-past-four-years/.

2*It's a Wonderful Life,* directed by Frank Capra (1946, RKO).

3*Rocky,* directed by John G. Avildsen (1976, MGM).

4Barna, *Growing Together* (Barna, 2022), 35.

5Barna, "New Research on the State of Discipleship," *Barna Group,* December 1, 2015, www.barna.com/research/new-research-on-the-state-of-discipleship/.

6Barna, "What Young Adults Say Is Missing from Church," *Barna Group*, November 13, 2019, www.barna.com/research/missing-church/.

7Eric Costanzo et al., *Inalienable: How Marginalized Kingdom Voices Can Help Save the American Church* (InterVarsity Press, 2022), 70.

[8]Tim Mackie, "Gospel Community—The New Testament," The Bible Project, December 1, 2018, audio recording, 9:50-10:23 and 8:33-8:47, www.youtube.com /watch?v=WqfeDTsPWVk.

[9]Dave Davies, "Trees Talk to Each Other. 'Mother Tree' Ecologist Hears Lessons for People, Too," *NPR*, May 4, 2021, www.npr.org/sections/health-shots/2021 /05/04/993430007/trees-talk-to-each-other-mother-tree-ecologist-hears-lessons -for-people-too.

[10]Robin Wall Kimmerer, *Braiding Sweetgrass* (Milkweed Editions, 2013), 21.

[11]Kelly Kapic, "Learning to Love your Limits," interview by Erin Straza, *Christianity Today* (January-February, 2022), www.christianitytoday.com/2021/12 /youre-only-human-kelly-kapic-limits-god-design/.

[12]Chris Whitman, "The Most Common Regrets People Have at the End of Life," Know Your Best, April 18, 2025, https://knowyourbest.com/common-regrets/.

[13]Liz Bohannon, "You Are Not Alone in Feeling Alone," Life.Church, October 15, 2023, Life.Church Message, 9:00-9:25, www.youtube.com/watch?v=aIIOn9rnxr4.

[14]Henri Nouwen, "January 23," in *Bread for the Journey: A Daybook of Wisdom and Faith* (Harper Collins, 2006), 23.

4. Know One Another

[1]Brené Brown, *Daring Greatly* (Penguin Group, 2012).

[2]John Lynch, "Two Roads," Trueface, March 13, 2012, video recording, 3:17-3:21, www.youtube.com/watch?v=Rfy03PEVUhQ&t=428s.

[3]Negar Ballard, "Over Half of Americans Report Feeling Like No One Knows Them Well," *Ipsos*, May 1, 2018, www.ipsos.com/en-us/news-polls/us-loneliness-index -report.

[4]Daniel de Visé, "A Record Share of Americans Is Living Alone," *The Hill*, July 10, 2023, https://thehill.com/policy/healthcare/4085828-a-record-share-of -americans-are-living-alone/.

[5]Hannah Anderson, "Oliver Anthony's Viral Hit Doesn't Love Its Neighbors," *Christianity Today,* August 17, 2023, www.christianitytoday.com/ct/2023/august -web-only/oliver-anthony-song-rich-men-north-richmond-love-neighbor.html.

[6]Barna, *The Connected Generation* (Barna Group, 2019), 22.

[7]Dietrich Bonhoeffer, *Life Together,* trans. John W. Doberstein (Harper Collins, 1954), 110.

[8]Barna, *Restoring Relationships: How Churches Can Help People Heal & Develop Healthy Connections* (Barna Group, 2020), 94.

[9]Brené Brown, "The Power of Vulnerability," TEDx Talk, Houston, TX, June 2010, 7:07-7:13, www.ted.com/talks/brene_brown_the_power_of_vulnerability.

[10]If this truth is difficult for you to accept, spend time absorbing God's Word, beginning with Ephesians 2:10. Psalm 103:11, Psalm 139:14, Zephaniah 3:17, and Romans 8:38-39.

5. Talk with One Another

[1]Jonathan Tjarks, "Does My Son Know You?," *The Ringer*, March 3, 2022, www.theringer.com/2022/3/3/22956353/fatherhood-cancer-jonathan-tjarks.

[2]Sherry Turkle, "Stop Googling. Let's Talk," *New York Times*, September 26, 2015, www.nytimes.com/2015/09/27/opinion/sunday/stop-googling-lets-talk.html.

[3]"American Time Use Survey," U.S. Bureau of Labor Statistics, accessed October 13, 2025, www.bls.gov/tus/.

[4]Data obtained in correspondence with American Time Use Survey (ATUS), U. S. Bureau of Labor Statistics, footnote M in ATUS, "Data collection issues in 2020 prevent the publication of 2020 annual, Q1, and Q2 ATUS estimates," www.bls.gov/tus/footnote.htm.

[5]M. Nolan Gray, "Why Dining Rooms Are Disappearing from American Homes," *The Atlantic,* June 10, 2024, www.theatlantic.com/ideas/archive/2024/06/dining-rooms-us-homes-apartments/678633/.

[6]"Mobile Facts Sheet," Pew Research Center, November 13, 2024, www.pewresearch.org/internet/fact-sheet/mobile/.

[7]Trevor Wheelwright, "Cell Phone Usage Stats 2025: Americans Check Their Phones 205 Times a Day," Reviews.org, January 1, 2025, www.reviews.org/mobile/cell-phone-addiction/.

[8]Derek Thompson, "Why America Is Suffering a 'Friendship Recession,'" *The Ringer*, November 29, 2022, www.theringer.com/2022/11/29/23483319/why-america-is-suffering-a-friendship-recession.

[9]"Revealing Average Screen Time Statistics," Backlinko, June 30, 2025, https://backlinko.com/screen-time-statistics.

[10]Peter Osborn and Eddy Canfor-Dumas, *The Talking Revolution* (Port Meadow Press, 2018), 1.

[11]Turkle, "Stop Googling. Let's Talk."

[12]Jackie Perry, "Why Good Listening Is Hard—And How to Get Better at It," March 6, 2025, in *The Care Ministry Podcast*, hosted by Laura Howe, published by Hope Made Strong, podcast, 7:30-7:45, www.hopemadestrong.org/podcasts/the-care-ministry-podcast/episodes/2148992213.

[13]Stephen Covey, *Principle-Centered Leadership* (Fireside Press, 1992), 45.

[14]"Adventures in Hosting," Living Room Conversations, accessed July 9, 2025, https://livingroomconversations.org/wp-content/uploads/2023/11/adventures-in-hosting-PDF.pdf.

[15]Ling Dinse and Tyler Gehman, "Living Out Colossians 4:6: The Practice of Constructive Conversations in the Classroom," *Biblical Higher Education Journal* 18 (2023): 11-32, www.abhe.org/wp-content/uploads/2023/04/2023.ABHE-BHE-Journal.pdf.

[16]David Brooks, *How to Know a Person: The Art of Seeing Others Deeply and Being Deeply Seen* (Random House, 2023), 72.

[17]Jeff Eberts, personal conversation with Phil Smith, February 2024.

[18]Latasha Morrison, *Brown Faces, White Spaces* (WaterBrook, 2024), 189-90.

[19]Martin Copenhaver, *Jesus Is the Question: The 307 Questions Jesus Asked and the 3 He Answered* (Abingdon Press, 2014).

[20]David Rock, "SCARF: A Brain-Based Model for Collaborating with and Influencing Others," *Neuroleadership Journal* 1 (2008): 3-4, https://schoolguide.casel.org/uploads/sites/2/2018/12/SCARF-NeuroleadershipArticle.pdf.

[21]J.R. Briggs, *The Art of Asking Better Questions: Pursuing Stronger Relationships, Healthier Leadership, and Deeper Faith* (InterVarsity Press, 2025), 130.

[22]Brooks, *How to Know a Person*, 43.

[23]Jonathan Tjarks, "Does My Son Know You?," *The Ringer*, March 3, 2022, www.theringer.com/2022/3/3/22956353/fatherhood-cancer-jonathan-tjarks.

[24]Aaron Earls, "Most Open to Spiritual Conversations, Few Christians Speaking," Lifeway Newsroom, February 22, 2022, https://news.lifeway.com/2022/02/22/most-open-to-spiritual-conversations-few-christians-speaking/.

[25]Bonnie Kristian, "Why We Don't Dump Friends Who Disagree," *Christianity Today,* July 7, 2021, www.christianitytoday.com/ct/2021/july-web-only/cancel-culture-why-we-dont-dump-friends-who-disagree.html.

[26]Brooks, *How to Know a Person*, 77-80.

6. Welcome One Another

[1]Trevor Noah, interview with Lesley Stahl, *The 60 Minutes Interview,* June 19, 2022, 5:30-5:35, www.youtube.com/watch?v=8_gyL3o6dIs.

[2]YouGov derived this data from a survey of 4,905 adults across the United States in December 2021. The Belonging Barometer was created by a research-informed, cross-disciplinary team to measure different experiences that affect how well someone "fits" or could potentially "fit" in a particular environment. Nichole Argo and Hammad Sheikh, *The Belonging Barometer* (American Immigration Council, 2023), vi, https://static1.squarespace.com/static/5f7f1da1ea15cd5bef32169f/t/641b16f74a75495c305d2625/1679496953766/The+Belonging+Barometer.pdf.

[3]Argo and Sheikh, *The Belonging Barometer*, vi.

⁴Bill Bishop, in his book *The Big Sort: Why the Clustering of Like-Minded America Is Tearing Us Apart* (Houghton Mifflin, 2008), was among the first to use the term "sorting" to refer to this phenomenon.

⁵Wellesley College, "New Study Finds Our Desire for 'Like-Minded Others' is Hard-Wired," ScienceDaily, February 23, 2016, www.sciencedaily.com/releases /2016/02/160223102840.htm.

⁶Joan Chittister, "Differences" in *Called to Community*, ed. Charles E. Moore (Plough Publishing House, 2016), 184.

⁷Michael Frost and Alan Hirsch, *The Shaping of Things to Come* (Baker Books, 2013), 68.

⁸John Ortberg, "Category Confusion," *Christianity Today*, June 14, 2010, www .christianitytoday.com/2010/06/categoryconfusion/.

⁹Josef Berthold, personal communication with the authors, May 25, 2025.

¹⁰Argo and Sheikh, *The Belonging Barometer*, 29.

¹¹Wellesley College, "New Study Finds."

¹²Glennon Doyle, "Horseshoes Are Better Than Circles," *Instagram*, April 27, 2020, www.instagram.com/p/B_f02wiD6DF/?hl=en.

7. Commit to One Another

¹National Retail Federation, "Convenience Is Driving E-Commerce Growth and Influencing Consumer Decisions," SmartInsights, January 28, 2020, https://www .smartinsights.com/ecommerce/customer-experience-examples/convenience -is-driving-e-commerce-growth-and-influencing-consumer-decisions/.

²Dietrich Bonhoeffer, *Life Together*, trans. John W. Doberstein (Harper Collins, 1954), 99.

³C. S. Lewis in a letter to Arthur Greeves, December 20, 1943, in *They Stand Together: The Letters of C. S. Lewis to Arthur Greeves (1914–1963)*, ed. Walter Hooper (Macmillan, 1979), 499.

⁴Timothy and Kathy Keller, *The Meaning of Marriage* (Penguin, 2011), 84.

⁵Isidore of Seville, as quoted in Mike Aquilina, *Friendship and the Fathers: How the Early Church Evangelized* (Emmaus Road Publishing, 2021), 191.

⁶Keller and Keller, *The Meaning of Marriage*, 84.

⁷Bonhoeffer, *Life Together*, 27.

⁸Jeffrey Hall, "How Many Hours Does It Take to Make a Friend?," *Journal of Social and Personal Relationships* 36, no. 4 (2019): 1278-96, https://doi.org/10.1177 /0265407518761225.

⁹Joel Eidsness, personal communication with the authors, October 21, 2023.

¹⁰Jennie Allen, "Why Am I So Lonely?," Life.Church, July 2, 2023, Life.Church Message, 22:40-22:55, www.youtube.com/watch?v=DNLX1hBEz-0.

Epilogue: Turning Back to One Another

[1]Malcolm Gladwell, *The Tipping Point* (Little, Brown, 2000).

[2]Maria Popova, "The Magic of the 'Trim Tab': Buckminster Fuller on the Greatest Key to Transformation and Growth," *The Marginalian,* August 21, 2015, www .themarginalian.org/2015/08/21/buckminster-fuller-trim-tab/.

Acknowledgments

[1]Drew Holcomb and the Neighbors, "I Like to Be with Me When I'm with You," by Drew Holcomb and Barry Jenkins, *A Million Miles Away*, Magnolia Records, 2009.